Dedicated to Alice & Don Nelson (parents & grandparents). You have always modeled a life of health and balance.

Always reminding us to make time for fun.

Thanks for supporting our dream.

Out of the lowest depths there is a path to the loftiest heights.

—Thomas Carlyle

Scottish Philosopher, 19th Century

ACKNOWLEDGMENTS

We thank Buddy Smith, husband and father, for his continued love and support. We thank Tom Poland and Kelly Allen, our editors for this project. We could not have pulled this off without their help. We give a big thanks to Alice Nelson for spell check and serving as grammar queen.

And we thank our friends in recovery. We would not be where we are today without your commitment to health and recovery. To all the therapists along the way, we extend our heartfelt thanks. We love therapy! And thanks to God for being sovereign and good.

INTRODUCTION

Our journey. The addict and the co-addict. He is my son and I am his mother. This is our separate journey to a world of health and freedom. We will each tell of our account of what it was like, what happened for us to want to change and what life is like now.

Grayson started drinking cough medicine at 14-years-old and by the time he was 15 he was taking pills, drinking, and smoking pot. I was at my wits' end trying to figure out what was wrong and how to fix it. His drug use increased rapidly and I'll never forget his phone call after what could have been a fatal car wreck.

We tried all kinds of things to help him: therapy, changing schools, self-help books, and stricter rules, but things only got worse. I got worse, consumed by awful thoughts of "what ifs."

We sent him to rehab and then watched him move out West at 20. I began to let go of him as my attention shifted to the needs of our middle son, also battling addiction. Our family was falling apart and I learned I was powerless over addiction.

In my desperate search for answers, I began to see what recovery for me would take. I walked back in on myself and took control of my life, and in time, began to heal. Grayson, in his own journey and desperation, eventually found recovery for himself. Be assured that writing this paragraph of sixty-six words, however, doesn't begin to convey the heartache, frustration, and struggle.

Our lives became unmanageable and at different points we surrendered to God and applied the twelve steps of Alcoholics Anonymous.

Today, we both enjoy the freedom that recovery brings. I live my life and recovery and he lives his life and recovery. Separately, we pursue physical, emotional and spiritual health. We do this one day at a time.

Taking Account Of Things (Grayson)

Ever since I can remember, I didn't fit in. Something was missing inside me. It was not obvious so I never thought I should mention it to anyone. Or maybe it was because my family didn't talk about emotions or show a lot of affection toward each other. For whatever reason, I was broken and it was up to me to fix it.

The first time I got drunk, my problems were fixed. I could talk to girls and joke around with other guys. I was a better athlete and felt much more fit when I was drunk or high. My hair looked better. Drugs and alcohol were the solutions to my problems. They put the color into my black and white world. I continued to search for better answers until I was a textbook heroin junky. I got really good at doing things I didn't want to do. Being dope sick was a normal part of my life.

At some point, my greatest asset turned against me. I was in a lot of debt, sick and smoked pot like other people smoke cigarettes. I drank all day. I was a nervous wreck. I had tried everything and nothing seemed to work. I had a solid 6 mg of Xanax dependency on top of countless other addictions. That one scared me the most. I knew withdrawals could kill me, especially combined with the alcohol withdrawals. I wanted to stop, but at this point it was far too late for me to accomplish that feat on my own.

I lost all the jobs I cared about. Somehow I managed to get hired on ski patrol in Mammoth Lakes, California. I also worked a few outdoor education contracts for a school in Santa Monica. During these trips, I was responsible for the safety and well being of a dozen high school kids in the wilderness. The truth is, the only thing I was responsible for was making sure I picked up enough heroin and cocaine to last me through those trips. No one had a clue. I'm sure they thought I drank too much at times, but cocaine and heroin? That is crazy. I was crazy and so full of shit.

I hung on to heroin and cocaine as long as I possibly could. While in college, I started to grow and sell pot to have a way to support such an expensive habit. It usually took about $100 a day on and off for five years. When I ran out of heroin, I would try to shoot up Benadryl, vodka, or that black crumb that sort of smells like heroin. I was addicted to the needle.

I got arrested for selling a couple grams of hash to an undercover agent. That was it for me. I was doped up at the time and didn't think too much of it. My girlfriend leaving me, getting kicked out of my house, and my dog dying had really raised my tolerance for emotional pain.

When it finally registered in my drug-addled brain what was about to happen—prison for three years—I was ready to take other people's advice. Maybe I didn't know everything. It became clear to me then that all these problems were of my own making and I needed help. I wanted treatment. I wanted to go now! I was desperate and I would do anything.

Childhood Trauma (Grayson)

There was something about me that was different from everyone else. I was gross. I was slow. I was awkward. Deep inside, I always knew this. I tried my best to forget it and at times I was really close to forgetting the darkest moments in my life. No matter how much I drank or used, I could not completely wipe my memory clean of the filth that was imbedded in who I was.

We are as sick as our secrets. When I was about ten-years-old, a family friend molested me. He was 16-years-old and I thought he was so cool. He played football and had a lot of friends. He also paid attention to me and would hang out with me after school. It made me feel special that he wanted to hang out with me. I was fat and my peers made fun of me. Hanging out with someone who was so cool and did not make fun of me was exciting.

One day we were at the pool in our apartment complex around mid morning. We were in the laundry room within the pool complex. I do not remember the whole experience and that is probably a good thing. I have heard people say kids have an ability to not remember traumatizing events in their childhood; it is a defense mechanism. I think I used mine that morning. What I do remember is Sammy's penis in my mouth. I remember being scared and confused. It felt wrong. I felt guilty. I did not want anyone to know what I had done.

It became true what everyone said about me. I was fat and clumsy. More than that, I was disgusted with myself. I shouldn't have done that. I wouldn't tell a soul about this experience until I was in my late 20's. I lived most of my life with an overwhelming sense of guilt, shame, and disgust. I absolutely hated myself for letting someone take advantage of me like that. I hated the way I looked and I hated the way I sounded. I was awkward and fat. I was sure that people could tell what I had done just by looking at me.

Drugs and alcohol temporarily relieved me from the guilt and shame that only amplified when I sobered up. This created a vicious cycle of self-hate and mental torture. I did not know how to deal with the gravity of it all. I began to tell myself that it really wasn't that big of a deal. I told myself that for years. I told myself it wasn't a big deal and I began looking for other things to blame my shame and guilt on. It was a big deal. I was only ten-years-old. I did not know how to stand up for myself. Especially to my coolest friend Sammy. It was not my fault. I needed to be honest with someone. I wanted to tell someone.

When I was 26, I got a therapist. She was drop-dead gorgeous and I was attracted to her. How could I tell someone I was so attracted to? I couldn't. I wanted to know if this traumatic event was causing a lot of my pain. I wanted some validation. I couldn't tell her. I never told her. This was becoming unmanageable, and at the time when I was seeing a therapist my drug and alcohol use was a means to live. I absolutely needed it to stay alive. I felt like it helped me breathe. It was more than just taking a little too much. I needed to drown myself. I woke up everyday feeling like shit and dreading having to be alive one more day. I drank and used in the morning before breakfast. I didn't have a choice anymore. That was a luxury long gone. I did it out of necessity. I did not even want to. The shame and guilt continued to build as I went against my word to myself, and I was trapped in a dark place with no way out.

§

Walking Miles - (Patty)

As a young girl, I walked all the time. Walking the many hills of my suburban Atlanta neighborhood was refreshing. Donning my sneakers, I hit the asphalt. Never knowing which street I might choose or how long it would be, I just walked. I gazed at all the tall southern pines and large magnolia trees, looking up at the sky and soaking in the sunlight. Once, I picked roses from a neighbor's bushes as I walked by. Letting go of life's problems as I moved and gaining a new perspective as I breathed. When walking, I had many conversations with God. We discussed all kinds of things, me sharing my hopes and dreams, struggles, and disappointments. Him giving me hope and reassurance, knowing He is sovereign and always good. I relied on this relationship to give fulfillment and purpose, finding answers to my questions and direction when I lacked clarity.

Today I continue walking and absorbing all the elements of nature (I'm a professed tree hugger) while conversing with God.

He meets me where I am and fills up my soul.

I tried, for a while, to have my needs met in family, only to be left empty and disappointed. God is my source of fulfillment and strength, helping me to be ok when things or people around me are not ok. He is my all in all and He is enough and I was going to need Him in the worst way.

§

First Drink (Grayson)

The first few times I got drunk it was clear I had a problem. I knew well before I took the first drink why I was going to drink. I just wanted to get drunk. I knew it would make me feel like a rock star. I knew it was the solution to my problems before I even tried it. My mind was made up a long time before I experienced the first drink. I think I was 14-years-old and my friend's older brother hid some gin in the woods behind his house. It was in a 20-ounce water bottle.

One Friday after school, my two friends and I were going to find it and pass it around a few times. This was my chance to fix the way I felt. I was so excited and it was all I thought about at school. I simply couldn't wait for class to be over so I could feel great. I knew it was going to be amazing. I was not patient. I was eager to find this water bottle and my friends knew I was excited. I was in a hurry, but they didn't seem to be in such a rush. They lingered after class and I wanted to run home.

We got to my friend's house and started our journey. We were walking casually to find this bottle that we hoped to find somewhere near a tree in the woods. I was out front walking much faster than the rest. I had a plan. I was going to drink all of it, so I tried to make sure I was in a position to do so. I knew they would be mad at me, but I didn't care. I would be drunk and nothing would matter.

Finally my friends shouted, "it's over there." Without missing a beat, I ran over to the bottle, opened it up and chugged all of it. I drank it so fast I didn't have time to throw up. I had been practicing in my mind how quickly I was going to drink it. I threw the empty bottle down and my friends started yelling at me. I didn't care; it felt like I drank a bottle of hair spray. I leaned over and let the saliva flow out of my mouth. I was fighting back the urge to vomit with all my might. My stomach was upset and did not want all that warm gin in it. My mind won that battle. I kept all the warm gin down and waited for the effects. They were almost immediate. I didn't give a fuck about anything. I was talkative and energetic. I was slim and attractive.

We were planning on going to a party at this popular girl's house and I couldn't wait. I was sure I would be more popular, because I was drunk and fun to be around. I don't think it worked out like that though. My friends had to babysit me to make sure I didn't say anything dumb or hurt myself. They were successful in the latter but I said tons of dumb shit and looked like a fool. We got back to my friend's house and I continued to be obnoxious. I peed on his floor and passed out right next to my puddle of urine. My friends were upset with me but I was in love. I had found my cure. This was only the beginning of peeing on floors, irritating my friends, and having others manage my life. I didn't see any of that in the beginning. It was all glorious. I didn't need friends like I needed alcohol.

5

Patty's Idol

When I was a little girl, I idolized Julie Andrews. I wanted to be her. I owned her record albums, "The Sound of Music" and "Mary Poppins." I would dance and sing all around the living room. The album covers were full of pictures relating to every song and I spent hours lost in make-believe. So, when I grew up and had kids of my own, naturally I believed they should be like the Von Trapp children or the Banks children. We would sing and dance our troubles away—Not! My vision of going on hikes through the meadow with a guitar in tow quickly evaporated in the world of reality. "I'm tired, I'm hungry," replaced the jovial laughter of my fantasy kids.

I did not give up. We went to the park a lot, and I substituted McDonald's playground for the Swiss Alps.

I bought lots of books just to quickly have them replaced by Game Boy. I put a lot of stock in being a Mary Poppins kind of mom, but I was losing.

Middle school took my kids away even further. They began experimenting with drugs and alcohol. Sneaking out of the house at the wee hours of the night was common.

This is not how it's supposed to be. This is not according to plan.

Prayer and journaling became a common practice for me. Crying out to God, " God help!" was often all I could express. Exasperated and weary, I plugged away. I learned a whole new skill set of administering drug tests in my kitchen. This is not normal, is it? What happened? Disney did not play out in my world.

Life was hard and I labored to breathe. My kids were going downhill fast. My sadness and heartache were unbearable. I remember walking into church after Grayson's car wreck and panning the sanctuary, looking for someone to confide in — someone safe to tell all I was going through, someone who would understand. I finally found someone to talk to who was understanding, but the truth is they didn't really understand.

I always felt lost and hurting right in the middle of church. I could hardly think straight and struggled to continue my daily duties. What in the world was I going to cook for dinner? I was often paralyzed. I was in pain with no one to comfort me. I learned years later, deep in my soul, that God would be that comfort, and I learned to be ok when those around me were not ok.

§

Car Wreck (Grayson)

It was the first time I was in a car that flipped over. I was 16-years-old, and I did not know it was the first of many wrecks to come. I was a freshman in high school and I could not wait to have access to guns, drugs, sex and my own money. Something inside me felt like I needed an advantage over everyone else. Something about me made me different, and I wanted to be one step ahead of the rest of the world. Drugs, alcohol, money, and women were going to be the answer. The first time I bought weed, I spent $40. The second time I spent $400. There was a direct correlation between how much pot I had and how many people wanted to hang out with me. I figured it out. If I had more drugs, I'd have more friends. This was part of my advantage over you.

My dad let me drive his Acura RL 3.5 when I got my learner's permit. It was black. I couldn't wait to put rims on it. I had plans for a sound system and many other additions that would make people want to hang out with me. I was certain my life was boring and no one wanted to be around me as is, so I needed to spice things up a bit.

It was so exciting to sneak out and go to parties with high school dropouts and others who were affiliated with gangs. I wanted a gun badly. I had started selling pot to my friends and felt like this was going to be the key to my happiness. I had "mentors" who taught me all about getting high and how to buy and sell drugs. My spare time was spent on Erowid or other websites that were cyber encyclopedias for everything related to drugs. I had found my bible and I was obsessed. I wanted nothing to do with you if you were not going to get high with me, and I was certain no one wanted to be around me unless I had access to said drugs.

One of my mentors, Brad, had endless amounts of Xanax and painkillers. He would meet me and sell me as many of his pills as I wanted for $5 a piece. These were just for me. I wasn't going to sell any of these; they were too precious to me and would remain my biggest asset for years to come. Brad used to take me to parties with college-aged kids and other high school dropouts. Brad had a gun.

Brad knew how to fight and stuck up for me. He was one of the first people I felt like I had a relationship with. He told me how to do cocaine and how to smoke crack ... something that would be a part of my life sooner than later. Sneaking out became routine. I would take Xanax and then I would be able to relax and drink like everyone else at parties. I was one of the last people awake still drinking and smoking with fewer and fewer people to indulge with me. I would hang out with anyone at that point if you would drink all night with me.

I would drive clear across town to party with someone I hardly knew just to not be alone. One night sticks out. I went to a friend of a friend's house. I knew who these people were but I was not invited directly by the person whose house it was. I had my Xanax and painkillers and a large bag of weed, plenty enough to make friends for the night. Plus I was driving a really nice car. I struggled to make conversations and felt that I didn't belong at this party. Everyone was laughing and dancing, and it looked fake. None of them looked like I felt inside-lost.

As the night dragged on, I continued to drink. I smoked cigarette after cigarette, joint after joint, and took lots of pills. I was told it was time to leave the party. It was around 2 a.m. and I sure as shit didn't want to go home. I hadn't reached my comfort level yet. I was certain I wouldn't be able to sleep if I went home. I met a guy everyone called "Snow" because of his gang affiliation and the fact that he was white. He was a loser. He was 17 and a high school dropout. He told me he knew of a party but it was kind of far away. "No problem," I said, "I can drive". Thank God I didn't need to go home.

We drove for about 45 minutes. I had to get gas. We were in unpopulated farmland in South Carolina. Everything was very spread out. As the road kept unwinding, I began to relax more into the leather seat of my dad's car. Snow didn't have a license so I had to drive. I finally felt stoned and drunk and my eyes got heavy. As hard as I tried, I could not keep them open. I would catch myself nodding out behind the wheel and it would scare me awake for a few minutes before it happened again. We stopped at a run-down countryside gas station run by an old lady who looked like she hadn't slept for days. Snow didn't have any money for gas. He didn't have anything to offer.

Why was I hanging out with this loser? What the hell am I doing an hour away from home? What the fuck are my parents going to think when they wake up and realize I'm not home? I will figure something out; right now I just need gas. I filled up my tank and got behind the wheel again. I was sure I was more awake now. I was wrong. I fell asleep behind the wheel at the gas station and apparently so did Snow because he didn't say anything. When I woke up, I told him he had to drive, that I was too tired and fucked up. Snow assured me he was fine to drive. As soon as I buckled my seat belt in the passenger seat of Dad's car, I let the Benzo-alcohol blanket take me. I was in a comfortable coma only to be rudely awakened by a violent swerve that pumped adrenaline into every part of my body and then glass. Lots of glass. And then what I thought was smoke, but it was the powder from the airbags. I waited for pain. I knew it always came after the adrenaline. It never came. I was fine, and so was Snow. We were upside down. We shimmied out of a window. No big deal. That was my first thought. I just needed a minute and I could figure out what to do. We will just flip the car over, drive to Snow's place and get the windows fixed tomorrow. Perfect. We had a plan.

Flipping the car over was easier said than done. I felt strong but not strong enough to flip over the crinkled black car that my dad let me use. I was fucked, but I wouldn't realize that for at least 10 more years. OK, plan b? We could walk back to the gas station, ask someone to pull us out of the ditch, drive to Snow's, and then get the windows fixed tomorrow. This time Snow said he could help me pay for the damage. For some fucked up reason I believed him, knowing that he had nothing.

We walked miles and miles in the dark to the gas station with the old lady. The sun was starting to come up and people were beginning their Sundays. As customers rolled in, we asked them if they could tow us out of a ditch. No one was willing to help us. I was hungry, starving actually. When had I eaten last? Forget about that right now. What can we do? Snow could call his parents. He called his mom. I heard her raspy cigarette voice over the phone, "What did you do; are you in jail?'"

"No" he replied. Then I heard a click. Snow called her worthless. I was running out of plans. I did have a big bag of weed and a few pills left — my lifeline. The whole world could be burning down around me but if I had some Xanax and weed, it was going to be a great day. Well, plan C? Let's walk back to the car and see if we can flip it back over. It was light out by this time, so maybe it would be easier in the light. I also had a case of

Budweiser in the trunk, and getting drunk usually helped me to figure these sorts of things out. I had no idea how severe the situation was.

We walked back to the car. My cell phone was dead, thank God, because I didn't want to tell anyone what just happened. That would make it seem too real. I needed to smoke some weed and figure this out. As we got closer to the car, a cop passed us, then we saw him pull over next to what appeared to be a horrible wreck. There were ambulances and a fire truck as well. Holy shit! It was my dad's car. Seeing it in the light was confusing.

My brain raced back to the weed I had in my pocket. I was at a safe distance to toss it and no one would know I ever had it, but why would I throw away my lifeline when I needed it the most? I decided to keep it and tied it to the drawstrings inside my shorts. As we approached the car, I got my story straight. I was driving because Snow didn't have insurance. We were going to get breakfast early in the morning before church when a squirrel ran out in front of my car and I swerved to miss it and over-corrected and the car just flipped over.

He believed me. Oh shit, what if they look in the trunk and find the beer? Thankfully they didn't nor did they want to speak to my parents. The tow truck came and he gave me his card and told me where to go when I wanted to get some of my things out of the car. Do you need a ride asked the police officer? Shit. We did need a ride, but I didn't want to get in the cop car with a bag of weed. I didn't have any options at this point and I was pretty sure I was not getting arrested. He was very polite. No breathalyzer sobriety test or even the slightest suggestion that maybe I was drunk or high. I guess it was working out pretty well.

We got a ride back to Snow's house. His parents were not there and it looked like they hadn't been there for weeks. His brother was sleeping on the floor of their empty trailer with a small blanket. He said I could help myself to something to eat and a shower. He had nothing to eat and no towels or soap. I lay down on the empty floor and attempted to sleep, hopeful that when I woke up I would figure out the missing piece to this puzzle and be able to explain this to my parents in the most strategic way.

I was tired to my bones but I could not escape the situation. I was pissed off at Snow, because he was home and nothing had really changed for him. I had totaled my father's car and there would be consequences.

As I lay there, I knew my parents would wonder why I wasn't at home, why I was hanging out with a high school dropout who I didn't even know his name and why the hell I was so far from home. I knew they would ask if drugs or alcohol were involved. I didn't expect that a simple "no" would end that train of thought. After the phone call, I had their sympathy for being in a wreck early in the morning. I told them it was scary but the police officer had been nice and that no one was hurt. They said that that's the most important thing, and that they would be there in about an hour. I didn't want them to see Snow and I didn't want them to come inside. I didn't want to throw away my weed and I definitely didn't want to give it to Snow. Fucking asshole.

They came to pick me up and we hugged. They said they were glad I was ok and asked again if drugs or alcohol were involved. I assured them beyond a shadow of a doubt that they were not. We went to get some things out of the car and the tow truck driver told me how lucky I was to be alive and without a scratch. Yeah whatever, how was I supposed to get the beer out of the trunk and into my father's Tahoe? I didn't know how, but I did it flawlessly. No one saw me get the case of beer into my father's car right at my feet.

We drove for almost an hour and they never saw it. I'm really good at this, I thought. We got home and I told them I was exhausted. I managed to get the beer up to my room and on ice. I had made it. I gave myself plenty of credit for my accomplishment and would enjoy some beers to celebrate. I was in the clear. No one had a clue what I had been through last night and how drunk and high I was. My parents had no idea I was actually out partying all night and not waking up early to get breakfast before Snow and I went to church. As I lined up empty Budweiser cans along my window I was very proud of myself and the lies I told. I was going to be great at this, probably too good.

I had my pot under my mattress, a dozen more cold beers, a full prescription of Ambien and a few Xanax. I felt untouchable. If there was someone who could ruin that feeling, it was my father. During this period of my life and most of my childhood, he was very angry. I thought it was normal for dads to yell. That is just what they do. It seemed unpredictable at times. This time, I guess you could say it was predictable he would be upset, very upset.

I told my parents I was tired and needed to go to bed early. I think my father felt like he was missing a part of the story or maybe he just wanted to check on me. I thought he was going to kill me. I actually thought he was going to hurt or kill me.

He came into my room and exploded. He lost control. It was frightening to say the least. I was half drunk and in a pretty good mood and then a moment later I was terrified. The feeling of terror escalated as he saw all the empty beer cans. He immediately looked under my mattress and found my bag of weed. There was nothing I could say. I was out of lies. I was caught. I had no more plans. My father was furious and his anger was not declining. My mother was worried for the safety of her eldest son. My dad yelled and yelled. I was so terrified that I don't even know what he said. I couldn't think. There was too much anger to think. I just watched. I watched him unravel.

He did not know how to handle this new information, that his oldest son was an alcoholic and a drug addict. He could not control his oldest son and that infuriated him. He proceeded to take my computer out of my room and at once asked for my cell phone. My life was over. I couldn't sneak out without a phone to call people and I couldn't do any more research about drugs without my computer. Shit. I had no more pot and no more beer. My father's anger trumps all highs. I was not feeling any more of the alcohol. And then I realized something. I was saved. I had nearly a month's prescription of Ambien. That stuff would totally remove me from my shitty reality. If I snorted a couple of those, I would be fine again.

My mother figured out how to calm my father down, I think. Or maybe he was just too tired to be angry anymore and had to recharge before the next event. All I wanted was for it to be dark and time for them to go to bed so I could pretend to take another shower and snort a couple Ambien. Things did not work out for me as I had hoped that night. I was caught and it was becoming clear to everyone that I had a serious problem. I did not think that I would be in a treatment center soon but I did know it would take a lot more than something like that to make me want to change. I was just getting started and had big plans for myself.

§

God Hears My Prayer (Patty)

I prided myself on being a good mother so why was my son so unhappy? He was smoking pot and drinking and hanging out with guys who were going nowhere. He had changed and I was worried.

We tried everything to get him to stop. We hoped church youth group, restriction, positive reinforcement, or therapy would do the trick. The therapist said he was a well-adjusted kid. (He was good at telling people what they wanted to hear.) Nothing helped as he only pulled away more.

While experiencing great pain and desperation I prayed to God, crying out for Him to get my son's attention, do whatever it takes, but keep him safe.

And that's exactly what happened. He was in a terrible car wreck and came away from it without a scratch. Surely this will get his attention. We drove far to pick him up and stopped by the mechanic's to see the totaled car and let Grayson retrieve his school backpack.

That evening, thinking he was up in his bedroom grateful to be alive and rethinking his current lifestyle, he was actually drinking beers he had smuggled home from the back of the wrecked car. My husband heard noise from his bedroom and went to check on the poor guy. When he saw him guzzling beers, he flipped out. In his anger, my husband started to remove everything from my son's room. We were at a loss in our desperate state.

We searched the Internet for treatment centers and found one in Arkansas. Our hope was renewed. Finally, something to save my son. We packed up and left within a few days.

Grayson begged us to give him another chance and did not want or need treatment.

Stopping off in Atlanta on our way, he nabbed some Hydrocodone from my mom's medicine cabinet and took them the remainder of the trip. He took so much that it made him sick to his stomach. I thought he had a stomach bug. I had much to learn about addiction. I thought I knew a lot about my son but the staff at the rehab said I only knew the tip of the iceberg. How can that be?

I will never forget dropping him off at Capstone. After we got him checked in, Grayson told me he didn't want a formal goodbye. So, I walked out of the office of the treatment center and left my 16-year-old with total strangers, putting all my hope in them to fix my son.

As soon as the door shut behind me I broke down crying. I was overcome with a sense of relief and sadness. At least I was leaving him in a place where I knew he would be safe for the next three months.

After arriving home and waiting a few weeks, I get the coveted phone call from Capstone when I get to hear from my son. We had just entertained company for dinner and I was holding on to a wine bottle with a small amount inside. I took the call from Grayson and he sounded horrible. I was devastated and overcome with grief. I hung up the phone and clung to the bottle of wine, frozen in pain. "What if he never gets better? What if he never loves You?" These were questions I was asking God while I was slumped in the couch clinging to the remainder of wine. In my devastation, I vowed to God to fast and pray in hopes to get the answers to my questions. So, the following day I did just that and in my petitioning I heard from God that I can experience peace and even joy regardless of Grayson getting better. I can experience a supernatural peace and joy regardless of my circumstances. This was a life-changing moment for me. I still had great sadness and grief but I also had hope. Hope for myself finding healing from the pain.

§

PC Mom (Patty)

My son was in rehab and I still had two middle school children at home and a husband to feed and care for. I was overwhelmed with my circumstances.

While visiting the beaches of South Carolina, I noticed a family with adult children playing bocce ball. Watching them joke and interact with one another left me longing for that experience with my family. Why can't we have what they have? They are not torn apart because of drugs. They are not arguing or absent. They are healthy, happy, and engaged. I longed for that connection with my family, wanting to put an end to the devastation that addiction brings.

I remember pulling up behind a car that had a bumper sticker—PC mom—announcing that the driver of this vehicle had a child who was a student at Presbyterian College. Why can't I be a PC mom? This is not fair. I want a normal, happy family. I wanted the pain to stop and deeply desired to be a PC mom.

What is wrong and how can I make it right? I read many books and went to therapy in hopes to fix the wrong in my family, all to no avail. I then learned to find the relief and hope I was searching for by surrendering to God and connecting with community. By surrendering my situation to God and finding a community of people who had a similar experience, I found what I needed.

This helped me to connect with God and that peace and joy that I yearned was available to me. I shared my pain and heartache with others. They knew the same pain. We were united together in our grief.

I learned to hand things over to God—Let go and let God—was the solution. And I did that with others who at one time also wanted to be a "PC mom."

§

Capstone- (Grayson)

I did not want to go to treatment. I did not want to stop getting high. I had first experimented with cocaine back home. It was incredible. I had learned a lot since my recent car wreck. I knew how to hide the cash I made from selling pot. I kept it tied to the drawstrings of my cargo shorts next to a Visine bottle of bleach for passing drug tests. I was invincible. It was hard to keep up with the lies about who I was hanging out with and what I was spending my money on but I was managing. Cocaine was helpful because it allowed me to talk to anyone no matter how much Xanax I took or how much I drank. I never understood why people did cocaine socially. I thought that was a waste. I would always go to the bathroom and do it alone. I didn't want you to know I had it because I didn't want to share. I passed many drug tests that I shouldn't have thanks to a couple drops of bleach in my urine. One day I think I stopped giving a fuck or maybe I couldn't see straight or maybe I just forgot to drop some bleach in my urine and my parents found out that I had failed a drug test for cocaine. I didn't care because I didn't think there was anything they could do. Wrong, I was a minor so there was plenty they could do.

I was going to get treatment. They told me that I was going to get treatment and I resisted. I did not want to go. They were desperate for a solution to my drug and alcohol problem (if you could even call it that). When I was high or drunk, I didn't mind the idea of rehab. When I was sober, I fucking hated it. I was scared. My emotions were a rollercoaster and I didn't know what I really wanted. I didn't want to need drugs and alcohol to be normal, but I couldn't conceive a world without them. They told me that dog therapy was a part of the program. I would do anything for a dog. Absolutely anything. I needed a friend. So I agreed to go. I also knew that we were going to stop in Atlanta to visit my grandma before we went and her medicine cabinet was always stocked. I figured I could stay high the whole way to Arkansas and then I would have a dog in three months.

At this time in my life, I was very depressed. My search for purpose and friends was proving to me that I had no purpose and I would never have friends. It was me against the world. My parents didn't even know what to do with me. The only thing I knew was how to stay high and that was my purpose. Drugs were my best friend.

We drove to grandma's house and thank God she had pills. Ambien and Vicodin. What a wonderful combination. I remember not caring how much I took and would take handfuls until I was sick. I was trying to escape my reality and it was hard to take enough pills to mask my feeling of worthlessness. Ambien helped a lot, but snorting it doesn't last very long, plus snorting Ambien first thing in the morning makes for a very confusing day. I don't remember most of the trip. I do remember that when I was high it was easy, when I was coming down it was hard and I tried to make everyone as miserable as I was. Somehow we made it to Arkansas. I had a lot more pills left and I knew they were going to search me. Throw them away? Hell no! I decided to take the rest and I wasn't concerned if it killed me, actually that sounded pretty nice-a great solution to my problems. So I took the rest. My parents left and I was alone. It was me against the world again.

§

Jump (Patty)

When my oldest son was at rehab, we went to visit him. We participated in several team activities with several other families. One of these activities was to jump off a 40-foot post, free falling to the ground. I was terrified. I climbed up this tall post and was strapped into a harness with a wire that would kick in at the last minute before touching the ground. The wire was on my back, so I did not have the security of seeing or holding on to the wire. Just jumping and trusting the contraption to save me. Despite paralyzing fear, I forced myself to move forward. I made myself leap and have "leaped" many times since.

I often reflect on that exercise and am able to push through scary situations in my life, trusting God to catch me. It also helps me to make myself move, to do something in my life that creates forward movement. To take the next right step, the step that's right in front of me.

Learning to trust. I remember a time when someone asked if I could ever trust someone in my life who had broken my trust. I may not be ready to trust certain people in my life, but knowing I can rely on God helps me to live empowered. I can move forward in my life resting in the fact that God is there to catch me every time. When gripped by fear it's important that I keep jumping.

Lessons From Capstone (Grayson)

After Capstone I could not wait to get high. There were so many drugs I had yet to try. I thought I knew a lot about drugs, but apparently I didn't know anything. I learned about smoking meth, ecstasy, and shooting up heroin. These were all things I could not wait to do. I learned about shooting up cocaine with heroin, that being the best combination. There were many combinations I couldn't wait to try. LSD and ecstasy. Mushrooms and ecstasy. Cocaine and mushrooms. There are countless combinations and drugs that I was dying to try.

The first day at Capstone, I met a friend, someone who was in the same situation as I was. His name was Tyler and he was a meth addict and a really good liar. We vowed to stay friends and play the game of recovery. We promised we would see each other after the three months and get high together. We agreed that we must do whatever it takes to get out of here as soon as possible.

This wouldn't be so bad I thought. We walked around the property and found some mushrooms growing on the ground. Maybe these will get us high ... We ate handfuls of those filthy mushrooms to no avail. We spent the next three months putting up with everyone's bullshit and swapping stories of our drug escapades. His were incredibly more interesting than mine.

He taught me how to superglue the flap on an ATM machine and wait for people to try and use it. They thought the machine was broke. He taught me to scrape the super glue off and voila. Their money was now my money. He taught me about Ketamine and how to shoot it up. He made clear one thing. Using a needle is the best. I simply could not wait to try it.

I would get so excited talking to him and others about drugs that it was worth my stay in the middle of Arkansas. Between that and my dog, Mr. Biggs, I was doing alright. I wanted my parents to feel like shit for all the trouble they put me through and I made sure to communicate that to them during my weekly phone calls. This was a waste of their money and my time. I couldn't wait to prove them wrong. My therapist at the program told me one day that I could never safely drink alcohol again. What the fuck, I thought! I'm not even 17! First of all I don't care if I drink it "safely" and secondly, fuck you. The nerve!

I made it through the three months hating most of it except for the two-week backpacking trip. That would be something I took with me for the rest of my life, a love for the outdoors and recreation. I'm fairly certain without finding that I would have killed myself one way or another.

Mr. Biggs was the greatest creature I have ever had the privilege of knowing. He was with me everywhere for the next 12 years. The Appalachian Trail. Classrooms. Graduation. Concerts. And jail cells.

He was my best friend.

After Capstone, I knew I wasn't going to be able to go back to my high school with all my friends. I would be going to a private Christian school. I was pissed. I wanted nothing to do with this goody two-shoe school. Where would I find drugs and alcohol? It would prove far easier than I thought. Private schools have better drugs.

I got high just a couple days after Capstone. Tyler would be proud. I had a really hard time making friends, until I took a few Adderall. All of a sudden people noticed me. I had something to offer. And the high lasted all day. I was doing magic tricks I taught myself when I was on restriction and making friends at a rapid rate. It reaffirmed that I needed drugs and alcohol to be accepted and the sooner I accepted that, the easier my life would be.

I got caught. I said how ashamed I was and that my life was really hard at a new school. I promised to never do it again. I got a slap on the wrist and a new car. I started to play football. I was good at it and my pursuit of drugs and alcohol slowed a little. I was captain of the football team, made good grades and even praised Jesus on the weekends.

I began looking for something deeper. I enjoyed psychology class. I enjoyed reading the *Bible* and trying to figure out what was going on when it was written. I wanted an answer for my questions of the afterlife. Salvation didn't make sense to me but I was sure it would if I pursued it. This proved futile and gave me no answers. No burning bush for me. I gave my life to this and got nothing in return. There was no answer in the scripture. There was no relief when someone laid hands on me and prayed. There were lots of pretty girls, though, and they seemed very interested in guys who were living like Jesus. I wanted to be happy. To fit in. To have a pretty wife and an easy life, but those things weren't coming to me quick enough.

In frustration, I pursued this lifestyle with more dedication. Maybe I wasn't trying hard enough. I should stop watching porn; that's probably what was cutting me off from the sunlight of the spirit. Nope, that didn't work either. I was still alone, broken, and worthless. I decided to go to a Christian college where I could really study some of these ideas and connect with other people that have it figured out. I remember one night being frustrated with all the bullshit answers I got from professors about what the afterlife is like and what the Trinity is. They don't know, I thought to myself. It is impossible to know these things, but they spoke with certainty and this was not ok with me.

I took a class on the beauty of God's creation. One of the assignments was how we, as the hands of God, could use nature as a tool for salvation in others. What a burden I thought. If there is a God, He sure as fuck doesn't need me to "translate" anything. He doesn't need me to point out his beauty. If it exists, then people will see it. If not, then they won't. I don't want to get in the middle of what He is trying to communicate. This assignment rubbed me the wrong way to say the least. It bothered me.

At least I had a clear stance on the topic at hand. I wrote exactly how I felt and was proud of my final product. I rarely applied myself 100 percent. I didn't need to. I turned in my paper, double-spaced, MLA format, and met all the expectations for length and citations. I got a B+. I expected to be told to re-write it because of what I thought about the class. My teacher pulled me aside after class. She told me that my paper was well written. She also said that if this is what I think, I should consider transferring to another school with secular views.

That was all I needed to hear. Fuck it. No one left to argue with. I had reached my conclusion and was ready to move on. I had missed out on a lot of drinking, drugging, and sex. I felt stupid for pursuing a religious lifestyle when I knew what I wanted after all. I wanted to party. I wanted to have sex and smoke weed during the week. I remember hearing my pastor preach about the horrors of college and all the lost kids who smoke and drink all day. That sounded fantastic to me. Sign me up. I knew exactly where to go - Clemson University.

§

A Bad Break At Clemson (Grayson)

Clemson was a little more challenging, but I still found it unnecessary to study. I didn't even need to attend a lot of classes. I could just show up for midterm and final. There was tons of booze and pot. A lot of girls wanted to sleep with me, one of whom was my resident assistant. Wow, this was it. This was what I was waiting for my whole life. I had friends who drank and smoked all day with me. A pretty girl who would have sex with me whenever and lots of parties.

The glamour lasted a couple of weeks. The parties became dull. The girl was annoying and wanted a relationship. I couldn't smoke enough weed. It wasn't that I couldn't find it; I simply could not consume enough of it. For some reason Xanax was hard to find and expensive. This was frustrating, I knew there were better drugs around but I had a hard time finding them. I bought some fake acid and spent all day pissed off trying to smoke enough weed to activate the LSD. It never happened.

I drank more and more and withdrew from my friends. I didn't want to party any more. I didn't want a degree. This was all pointless. I didn't want anything. I had a lot of options, being as young and bright as I was, but I didn't want anything. I didn't want to come over; I didn't want you to come over. I didn't want to go to the lake. I didn't want to tailgate. It was all boring to me. I wanted to live in a hole underground and stay high. I would rather be alone and stoned than do anything else with anyone. Depression was a normal feeling now, and I didn't want anyone to know I felt that way. I thought if I didn't address it, it would go away. Plus I didn't have a good reason to be depressed. I was just maladjusted to life and hadn't found anything to be excited about.

I talked to a friend about rafting. That sounded exciting, a casual lifestyle where drinking and smoking pot were nearly a part of any guide job. No more formal education. Just live in a tent by the river and sleep with many of the college-aged clients who were just looking for a fun weekend. I found something to be excited about. I wanted to move out West and start a new life. I grew up playing in rivers. I'm a water boy. Always was and always will be. My mother likes to tell everyone that when I was a baby she dunked me under water and I would hold my breath. She wasn't going to raise kids that didn't know and enjoy how to swim. I love it. I love the swift water.

I did my research. I found a place where I would be trained in two weeks. I called a place in Washington—the farthest place from home and my depression. They were willing to hire me if I drove across country. Perfect. I fantasized about how wonderful my life was going to be. I fantasized about my new friends, the parties, and the fictional girlfriend who was waiting for me all the way across the country. I made it to the end of the semester with decent grades. Something happened though.

Two weeks before the semester was over, I broke my collarbone on a bike ride. Snapped like a dry piece of wood. I knew exactly what happened when I tried to pick up my helmet. I was crushed as soon as I realized what I had done. This meant no rafting. I held back the tears, not from the pain but from the disappointment. I told my friends to take me to the hospital. They insisted I was fine. I told them I would hit them with my good arm if they didn't take me immediately.

After the X-ray, the nurse said it looked good and I would be ok. That gave me false hope. Between that and three shots of morphine, I had hope that my life would be ok. That was until the doctor told me I needed surgery. The warm blanket of opioids left and I lost it. My life was over. I was sobbing. My hopes and dreams were dead. I had no plan and no purpose any more. My fantasy was dead.

I did get some pretty strong painkillers. This was it. I had a Vicodin and Percocet for the day and another painkiller mixed with a hypnotic to help me sleep with the excruciating pain. I was set to forget rafting, to forget college. I just needed more of these pills. I spent most of the days drooling on myself and telling everyone that these pills didn't work. I called the doctor and expressed my discomfort. He refused to give me any more—it had only been three days. Fuck you then. I will go to another doctor. The next day I was in another doctor's office and she understood me. She believed that I was in terrible pain and needed stronger medication. Thank God. She prescribed me enough opiates to knock out an elephant twice. Plus, I had everything from the previous doctor. I knew I could make a lot of money selling them to my friends, but I desperately needed them, so that was out of the question. With a little pot, some booze, and a few of my life-saving opiates, I could face any situation with confidence. I could handle things. My life was finally manageable. I would party with friends and take my nighttime meds during the day. I usually passed out within an hour of taking one of those pills. Then I would wake up at odd hours wondering how I got to bed. Why was the bed wet? I woke up with candy in my mouth and full beers spilled all over me. It wasn't embarrassing. It wasn't anything. I was cut off from any sort of reality and that was fine with me.

The morning after one of these experiences, I awoke to someone banging on my friend's apartment door. I was fully clothed holding a full beer that I somehow managed to not spill as I slept through the night. How rude, I thought. Why are they banging the door so violently? It was 2 p.m. but I didn't know that. I opened the door and was shocked. My mother! Oh shit! There was nothing I could do. There was far too much to try to hide. I did not let her in. She came in.

"Hi Jon," she said to my friend. And then she looked at me and said we need to talk. She told me she was scared for my life. That seemed a little dramatic to me. She said people died all the time from mixing opiates with booze. Also dramatic.

The truth was that I was unhappy. I didn't have a lot in common with my friends outside of getting fucked up. I wasn't remembering most of the good times. I suppose it was time for a change. It was her idea. She knew that I wanted a change of environment. She said I need to get out of here, away from these friends and this lifestyle. I agreed but for different reasons. For the first time in my life I was addicted to painkillers, and I didn't like needing them. It takes away a lot of the fun when drugs are a necessity rather then a luxury. I told her I would leave soon. I knew no one out West and had no real plans. I just wanted to go to prove to myself that I could do something. To prove to myself I could make friends if I was desperate. To prove to myself I could stop taking so many pills. To prove to my father I could get a job and make some money. I sure had a lot to prove!

§

Getting Better (Patty)

I began to get better and heal. Little did I know that Grayson was getting worse. He took off and moved to Colorado. I was very supportive. I felt he needed to get away and have his own life. Looking back, I believe he was running away and wanting to isolate. I wanted to see him go after something and have a happy life.

In my own journey of recovery, as I was getting healthy, I began to notice my unhealthy coping, recognizing ways I would give away my power to others. Learning that I can leave a room and have healthy boundaries with others was revolutionary. I saw how I over-functioned for family members and "helped" someone just to relieve my own anxiety. I began to see my health and unhealthy ways more clearly. This enabled me to live freer and to take better care of myself. I began to feel empowered. I would get phone calls from my grown children in distress and I learned to say, "I know you know what to do. I know you'll figure it out." I was empowering them to take responsibility for their own lives. I was able to take better care of myself when I let others take care of themselves. I was able to respect their struggle and allow them the dignity to fail. Freedom resulted from my new behavior.

§

Kingsley (Patty)

Shortly after my oldest son went to rehab, my husband and I were on a business trip to Arizona. Upon arriving in Arizona, I was struck by a culture that places emphasis on creation, a worshiping of the physical elements in nature. I found myself struggling and conversing with God, asking to see someone who worships the creator and not creation. Not giving my prayer much thought, I walked to breakfast. As I traveled through this ornate hotel and down a wide, fancy hallway, I saw and heard someone singing. I walked toward this man singing, thinking the music was the most beautiful sound I had ever heard. Though unable to make out any words he was singing, only the melody, I felt transported to a different dimension, just this angelic creature and me. I walked up to this man and words came spilling out, "Who are you worshiping?"

"The King of Kings, the Lord of Lords," he said. We shared a moment, exchanging names and occupations. Kingsley, from Jamaica, who works for the hotel told me that everything would be ok. God's in control. Experiencing the greatest comfort and awe over the transcending music I just heard, it took me a moment to realize my prayer had been answered and I felt God's great care. God was personal and real, answering my plea and giving comfort to my soul and its heartache. Kingsley's voice and reassuring words of hope, I knew, were gifts from God.

§

A Tearful Drive West (Grayson)

I cried most of the 26-hour drive to Colorado. I had Mr. Biggs, four-years-old now, with me and it didn't bother him one bit that everything I had was in my car and that I was leaving everything familiar. My mother was very supportive and for that I am grateful, but she still didn't understand the emotional turmoil I was going through. No one did. Being alone in a car driving to a place I didn't know made the loneliness that much more powerful. I had a few pills and plenty of weed. I had to take the pills strategically to get me to Colorado. I couldn't take them all too soon or I was sure I wouldn't make it.

I wanted to turn around so bad. This was absurd, I thought. This was not going to fix me, nothing would. I was broken and shattered into a million pieces. I couldn't remember a time when I was ok. This was all I knew and it was exhausting. I needed friends. I needed someone to understand me for once. I needed answers that had nothing to do with God.

My mom talked too much about God. I think she still does. You know what really frustrates me? God's will. God will take care of his children. God has a plan for you. I heard God say ... All those comments make me want to explode. How can God actually give a shit if I feel like this and he has never done anything about it despite my desperate search for an answer? How are my parents so foolish to believe in a loving God? They are educated people; it made no sense to me. It still irritates me. I'm fine with being a little irritated these days though.

The hole inside me was not getting any smaller as I drove closer to Colorado. I had an unrelenting feeling of impending doom. I was going to get in a wreck and die. My dog was going to run away. I was going to get pulled over and arrested for possession, which is actually surprising that that didn't happen. I watched the clock and made sure to smoke every hour. Early in the trip, I made a point to pull over and smoke outside my white Ford Explorer, which would be home for the next few weeks. Then I decided it was safer to smoke inside my car. Then I was so paranoid, I would change my mind constantly switching my methods. There's not enough Febreeze to mask that smoke. Eye drops did not clear my eyes from crying and smoking. I was a wreck and I didn't know what I was doing. I called my mother and expressed my concerns. She encouraged me to keep going.

I was searching desperately for something to make me whole for once. At night, I would drink excessively and watch movies on my laptop in the back of my Explorer with my dog. I had a black futon mattress that fit perfectly in the back. I would not have made it to sleep if it wasn't for the booze. It gave me a moment to recharge and repair the damage I had done to my psyche during the day. I didn't know it at the time but I was tearing myself up with comments about how ugly I was. How uncoordinated. I replayed all the hurtful moments of my childhood in hopes the anger would give me strength to change. I continued to engage myself in negative and hurtful comments all the way to Colorado.

I knew no one here. The only thing I remember was seeing a picture of Rocky Mountain National Park in a Backpacker magazine. It looked so peaceful. It was much bigger than my problems and me. In the presence of those peaks, I was certain, my problems would dissolve. So I punched Rocky Mountain National Park in my GPS and off I went. I had big plans to get to the top of as many peaks as possible. I had $2,000 from my grandparents who desperately wanted me to live right down the road from them. The irony, however, is that though they wanted me to stay, their money helped me go.

I passed through the entrance gate to the Rocky Mountain National Park with no map and minimal camping equipment. I was ready to suffer more. I deserved it. The ranger explained to me that dogs were not allowed on any of the trails and must be leashed at all times. What? I can't hike with my dog? I drove 1,600 miles to hike around and I can't?

I swallowed my frustration and found a campsite. I needed to drink and smoke and figure out my next move. I spent the next three days at my campsite smoking and drinking and being nervous someone was going to arrest me. Mr. Biggs did not mind one bit that we couldn't hike together. He was perfectly content lying on the ground and watching me smoke and drink aggressively, hoping to fill the dark hole in me. This was part of the reason I loved him. He was always ok. He was always at peace. He had the sweetest eyes that always expressed his love for me. He was creative, too. I would spend hours watching him watch wildlife. He desperately wanted to catch a squirrel. I wanted to let him try because I knew he would never catch one, but I was too scared to get a ticket to let him off the leash.

One night as I was preparing my Chef Boyardee on my green Coleman stove, Mr. Biggs was scheming. I did not see the family of mule deer grazing right next to our campsite. Mr. Biggs saw them. He remained quiet. He knew he wasn't able to chase anything when he was tied up so he began to chew through his leash. He had done this before. He chewed through his leash and took off like a lightening bolt. One minute he was half asleep, and the next minute he was tearing through the campground barking and hollering at the innocent deer. He was in heaven and for the first time in months I laughed. I laughed so hard. It was refreshing to see him so wild.

My laughter stopped when I saw the park ranger quickly walking over to my campsite. "You need to leash your dog," said the ranger. I replied that he was on a leash but he had chewed through it. I knew I wasn't going to catch my dog. He would come back when he was done and he did. The park ranger scolded me and did not write me a ticket. For a few minutes that night I was able to escape my hopeless situation and enjoy being where I was.

I felt that my time in Rocky Mountain National Park had come to an end and I should begin to pursue friendship. My time isolating in the wilderness left me somewhat refreshed from all the driving and crying. The air was cool and I was in a new and exciting environment. My fantasy of new friends and a new life seemed plausible once more. I drove to Boulder.

I had no idea what to do when I got there. I began to unravel. I had no one. Just my dog that was making things very difficult. I couldn't stay in the hostel or most hotels with him. I needed a place to sleep. That was my next step. Just to find a place to get drunk and pass out. After that, I would have the energy to find some friends. I stayed in the cheapest hotel I could find. There I was, all alone clear across the country in a hotel room with my dog. Talk about being lonely. I was never one to watch TV all day; it makes me depressed. But I needed a distraction, so I watched as much TV as possible and got wasted. It was the best way to fix the horrendous problems with myself.

I knew I had problems, but I didn't know exactly what they were. I hated the way my voice sounded. I hated the way I looked in pictures. I hated the fact that at one point in time I was religious. I hated the cross tattoo I had on my shoulder. I hated myself. It was more than that though. I was a failure. I hadn't done anything with my life. I blew all my extra cash on drugs and alcohol. I needed to change. I needed to exercise, but I was too depressed to do anything about it. I was stuck.

I spent a few days on Craigslist looking to rent a room in a house that would be a great way to meet like-minded people. I chose to land in Boulder because everyone was young and happy. They all rode bikes. The hiking trails were always packed with happy couples and their dogs. This is where I could find salvation. I found an affordable room and went to meet the tenants.

I walked through the door and immediately knew this was the spot for me. There were bikes, hammocks, houseplants, and three huge bongs on the coffee table. Not one, but three intricate and detailed bongs, all for very different occasions. I was elated. There were Frisbees and longboards. Someone just finished making breakfast and offered me a cup of coffee. They were so nice and accepting. Most importantly they loved Mr. Biggs. He was a charmer after all. We spent the next couple hours smoking pot and talking about mutual interests.

They were curious. "What brought you to Colorado?"

"Well, I just got tired of the South and church," I told them. "I wanted to be in a place where I could hike, bike, and smoke weed." They told me of all the wonderful shows on the weekends and the numerous hiking trails. I couldn't wait to start my new life. They were impressed with the quality of weed I brought from South Carolina. They didn't think we had good weed in the South. I was pleased to pack bowl after bowl after bowl. I could have sat there all day talking to my new best friends but they had class and work. We talked lease terms and I told them I would get some money together and come back tomorrow. They said I could move in immediately.

I was so excited. It was like I found a shortcut to the cool kids. They were all good-looking, four out of five were in a band, and one had a beautiful girlfriend who walked barefoot everywhere and didn't wear a bra. I wanted this life. Finally, things had turned around for me.

I was the shit. Look at what I had done. I was brave enough to drive across country and pursue something I wanted and I got it. I was so proud of myself. I was fooling myself but I didn't care. At least I felt better. For a short time my drinking slowed down and I smoked like a chimney. I embraced the idea of marijuana being a medicine and a gift. I spent hours on their couch rotating between the three bongs, smoking with any fortunate soul that walked through the door. I had no job, so my days looked like this: Wake up early, walk my dog, make coffee and oatmeal, and sit on the couch smoking, waiting for my roommates to wake up. As they woke up, I would smoke with them. They would all leave for work or school and I was alone again. Smoking and smoking.

I was alone on the couch smoking one day and this joyful Asian character walked right into our living room. No one knocked at this house. The door was always unlocked and everyone was welcomed. I liked that. Dave and I became instant friends. He showed me around Boulder. He took me to the parks and would smoke weed with me all day. He had class, too, but it didn't seem to take up too much of his time. We spent all day hiking with Biggs and smoking pot. Finally, I have a best friend. I had never had a best friend that was human. Dave liked to drink a little more than me. Perfect. It made my drinking not look so bad. This was going to work out great.

I began looking for a job, my confidence was returning, and I was going to put it to good use. I immediately got a job at a calzone place. Soon I would become the manager. Me? A manager? That's crazy. As manager and pot connoisseur, I encouraged everyone to come to work stoned and to take regular smoke breaks to stay focused on customer satisfaction. We were making calzones for god's sake. We must stay high. Soon, I was bringing cases of beer to work to manage the 12-hour shifts.

When depression and feelings of worthlessness came back, I reminded myself of my accomplishments — that I was managing a pizza restaurant, had made friends, had moved to Colorado, and was paying rent. My partying escalated to new levels. My roommates liked to stay up all night at shows and after parties. I was beyond excited. We could walk or ride bikes everywhere. Finally my drinking and driving problem was solved. I could get filthy drunk and walk and that I did.

Mushrooms and ecstasy started to become a regular occurrence. I was exposed to new and interesting music like Sound Tribe Sector Nine where the first time I took acid was also the first time I took Molly, and I took more than one hit of each. I was in a spiritual place for that show. I was overwhelmed with serotonin. I could no longer dance. I was in a different world.

Things were so fresh and exciting to me and I needed to sit down and absorb the messages. I spent most of the Sound Tribe concert sitting down unable to converse with my friends. I was not able to smoke pot. Literally, all I could do was smile and look at the lights. I was so distant and felt like I had figured out something vital to my existence. I tasted something I thought was true. The universe accepted me and everything I hated about myself was part of me and what made me unique.

Psychedelics helped me accept who I was and that I knew nothing about life and God. I had countless deep conversations with strangers about the meaning of life. I was on a spiritual journey. This was it. I found the key to life. I thought I could stay in that spot forever. I didn't need to sleep again. I made sure to tell all my new friends that I loved them. I really loved them. And they told me they really loved me.

It all ended too quickly. The music stopped and I had to drive home. Holy shit. I have to drive home. I tried to explain to others that I was much too distorted to drive. They assured me they would help. We wouldn't listen to music on the way home and everyone would pay attention. Ok, I thought. We are all in this together. By some miracle of God, we made the 45-minute drive back to our house where we smoked pot until the sun came up. These were my people and I felt accepted and appreciated.

The confusion that followed such a profound spiritual experience is hard to describe. I lay in bed for as long as I could. The hunger started to hurt in my stomach but I had no appetite. I needed to go to the grocery store. My brain felt like it was scattered into a thousand pieces all across the world. I was exhausted from thinking about life and everything spiritual.

I managed to get myself to the grocery store. The confusion got more and more problematic as I strolled the aisles in my pajamas and slippers looking for something to help me. I had thoughts and then forgot them in the same instant. I would make up my mind and then forget what I just decided. This was frustrating. I wanted to be back in my bed where I could hide under the covers. I knew I needed to eat something, anything. I got the only thing that looked appetizing to me—three boxes of gushers. I ate them all and went to sleep. Had I done more damage than good? I couldn't think about that. I hung onto the feeling that I had finally found an answer to this fucked-up world and couldn't wait to visit that spiritual place again.

§

Pass The Mashed Potatoes (Patty)

When my oldest son was at rehab, I learned to communicate without getting emotionally charged. After delivering consequences to our teenage children, I would follow with a "pass the mash potatoes" attitude in order to move on. This exercise helped me to lessen my own reaction to the situation. If things got more heated, I would turn to my husband and ask if he would like to take a walk or go to the store. That kept me from getting caught up in the drama.

Living in a way that I could respond and not have to "react" to situations helped keep the emotions under control. Empowered in my relationships, I no longer took the bait. When invited to ride the crazy train, I declined. I detached from the craziness of others and detachment with love allowed me to care for my loved ones and not be a caregiver. I show love but I don't enable the addict. One time, for instance, instead of giving my son money, I delivered homemade soup to him. I was clear and stated my truth. I spoke up for myself, not speaking in code but saying what I meant simply and clearly. I controlled my emotions and actions and chose my words wisely.

§

No More Berating (Patty)

As I delved into my own recovery, I was reminded of a time years ago when a person berated me. I just sat there and took it. I froze in disbelief and shock as this person flung verbal insults my way. It hurt. It never occurred to me to get up and leave the room. I felt compelled to sit and take the abuse, since the person insulting me was "older and wiser."

When I began recognizing healthy behavior for myself, I knew I had been giving my power to others. No more. Now I politely get up and leave, a novel act that empowers me to take a stand when necessary.

As I got healthier, I could tell if someone was a safe person to interact with. I have choices I never knew I had as relationships go, and today the most important relationship I have is the one I have with myself.

§

Boulder Living, Then To The Appalachian Trail (Grayson)

This was the darkest of the dark times. Boulder was where I wanted to stay. I managed to get off pills for a short while and replaced them with booze, copious amounts of marijuana, and lots of psychedelic drugs. I was searching for a spiritual experience. I was desperate for it, and I found that when I took psychedelics. I felt like I was a part of something big and important.

Selling these substances was a noble cause in my opinion. I took a lot of pride in being an honest and caring dealer of these spiritual chemicals. It was short-lived. I have many fond memories of Boulder and I learned a lot about growing pot and selling it. I spent all my time and energy learning about pot and saving money to buy large quantities to sell to my friends in South Carolina where I could make $1,500 a pound. I thought this was my purpose in life and I was good at it. I was making a considerable amount of money and smoking pot that cost me very little. As a result, I stopped pursuing things that I had great passion for. Rafting and mountain biking could wait; I was in pursuit of some cold hard cash.

This lifestyle was not easy-go-lucky very long. It became stressful real fast and I never seemed to make as much as I wanted to. I had fewer and fewer friends to connect with and everyone soon became a resource to expand my small business. I was empty and I was sure if I could make a little bit more then my feeling of inadequacy would diminish. I had pain from my childhood that I desperately wanted to forget. LSD and ecstasy helped me cope for a few hours on the weekend, only to leave me in a darker place more alone then ever.

Where was God? He surely had no role in my life; neither did the rest of my family. I wanted nothing to do with people who believed in God or anything spiritual. I knew it was all bullshit and I tried to do my own thing. Me against the world.

Nothing helped. I became more alone and desperate for a spiritual experience. I had decided that if I really searched, I would have a spiritual experience. The connections I made in Boulder were wonderful. I met some amazing friends who helped me out and cared for me. But I was always left alone with a feeling I did not want to be with. I began to think about what I could do to relieve my pain. I decided that I would take my pain to the woods and find some answers and get some confidence. Hiking the Appalachian Trail was something I had wanted to do since I was in high school. I really thought completing the 2,165 miles from Georgia to Maine would make me a different person. After one last hurrah, I packed my things and loaded Mr. Biggs into the back of my Explorer for yet another trip cross-country. I was desperate for change.

§

Coffee Scoops (Patty)

When I was a girl, I loved my stuffed animals. I would put all of them on my bed, which served as our boat. We would travel the seas and I would care for all the animals. I would mark them with a red magic marker for blood and then bandage their wounds with great care. "Helping out" was what I loved doing. My dad often told me that I could not save the world, but I kept trying. I have a knack for anticipating others' needs. This gift can also be a curse.

I also found it natural to interject my helpfulness when my parents had an argument. I would point out to each of them what the other really meant to say. "Mom is really saying this or what Dad really means is that." I put myself right in the middle and triangulated. This skill of mine carried through to adulthood, where I practiced it on my husband and kids. I would mediate conflict when it was not even my conflict. While trying to be helpful, I often made situations worse.

In recovery, I learned to respect the struggle of others and the struggle between others. One day, while trying to perfect my skill and mind my own business, I was making coffee in my kitchen as my husband and daughter were having a disagreement. Struggling not to add my commentary, I decided to count coffee scoops out loud, "One, two, three …" This vocal declaration of scoop counting helped me stay out of their way, letting the two of them work out their own conflict. Victory. I was learning a new, healthy behavior. It was liberating. Learning to be ok when others were not ok. Respecting the struggle and allowing others the dignity to fail helped me to grow. Scooping coffee out loud was the key for me.

§

Hiking The Appalachian Trail (Grayson)

I saved some money working at the pizza restaurant, but I was going to need some more. Plus I was going to need a lot of weed for my six-month journey so I spent every last dollar I had on a large quantity of grade-A cannabis. It was expensive but it was the best around. I went to my friend's recording studio to pick it up and I was intrigued. He clearly had a lot of money and a lot of cannabis. I saw the correlation.

I was excited and nervous to drive this much pot back to South Carolina but if I could tough it out for a couple of days, the payoff would be worth it. I was a nervous wreck driving a few hours, and then getting drunk at night so I could sleep. To say it was stressful is an understatement. I passed cop cars and stood behind police officers in line at the gas station. I kept an outward appearance of calm, something I had taught myself at a very young age, and it seemed to work very well. No one had any idea what I was doing and I did not know that this secret was actually making it worse.

I called up some friends and in a couple of days, I had made back the money I spent with a ton more marijuana still to sell. I had made a good investment and I was proud of myself. I was going to triple my money. I also made everyone very happy. Marijuana of this caliber is very expensive in South Carolina and it has a tendency to sell itself. All I had to do was put it on a scale and do some math on my phone.

I was making money and spending it on cocaine, nice booze, and whatever else I thought would make me happy. I was having a blast and distracted from the pain.

I remember taking my box of cash to the bank at Clemson University. I sold the remainder of my pot at Clemson. I kept some for myself and I kept some cash in my car just in case and because I liked to count it. It fed my ego.

I told the lady I needed to make a cash deposit and she asked how much. I said $9,000 and she didn't know if I was joking or serious until I opened my small box on the counter. I knew that if I deposited more than $9,999 it would draw too much attention. I told her I had been working in the food and beverage industry and had been collecting my tips all through high school and college. No big deal. Man, I was proud of myself. I had money in the bank, cash in my car, a few ounces of weed for myself, and extraordinary plans to hike the trail and find myself.

I stuck around town for a few days collecting other drugs that would make my experience easier. I had a lot of cash and I spent it all on drugs. I told myself I would only buy a gram of cocaine and then I would see how much the dealer had and give him an offer for the rest of it. A few minutes later, I would spend half my money and have plans to make it back by selling the discounted cocaine. I could never just buy a little bit. If I saw some sort of deal, I took it and helped myself to the drugs.

I bought an assortment of pills, Adderall, Benzos, and a vile of acid, plus I had two ounces of weed for the trail. Weren't my intentions to hike the trail somewhat sober? When did I make the decision to bring all these substances? Shit, this was not part of the original plan. I started to feel shame associated with not being able to keep my word with myself, something I would later learn to be my greatest asset. I quickly tried to stop this internal conversation in hopes of not making me feel any worse.

My father dropped me off north of Blue Ridge National Park because dogs were not allowed in the park. This was supposed to be exciting and happy. I was terrified and very sad. I was not motivated and I was literally all alone in the woods with all my pain. This was overwhelming but I still didn't want anyone to know. I kept a smile on, told my father that I loved him, and thanked him for the ride. He had no idea what my last few weeks were like. All I wanted to do was get to a spot where I could smoke myself into oblivion and wake up the next morning hopefully with some motivation to hike 2,160 miles alone.

I was not able to finish the trail. I hiked slow, drank a lot and stopped at every chance I got to party with whomever I could. I made some great memories and it sounds good on paper, but what no one could see was that I was totally broken and all my plans to fix myself were failing. I began to feel like I had a serious, permanent problem. I couldn't sleep and I was never happy or interested in anything.

I went to a doctor in Connecticut to try to get some sleeping meds. I wanted benzos and mine had all run out. He had a sign on the wall: "The only two people who care enough for you are Jesus and the Marines."

"What the fuck?" How did I end up finding this bozo doctor? This had to be illegal somehow. But it wasn't. I told him I could not sleep. He asked me if I was getting enough exercise and I told him that I hike about 20 miles a day. I told him I have had trouble sleeping since high school and the only thing that works are benzos. I was desperate and I paid a lot of money to see this clown. He told me he was not comfortable prescribing those. I told him I spent a lot of money to come see him, that I couldn't see my other doctor and I would appreciate a months supply. He agreed.

I was saved for a few more days. I was fine again, I knew everything would be ok with a bottle of Klonopin and I joyfully strolled to the pharmacy. I also figured out that libraries were where homeless people spent their days and they also had pills. So, I would hang out at libraries and let it be known that I had great pot and would trade it for some pills.

I was back into pills harder than before and they really helped. They helped me breathe. Without them, I felt like I would suffocate. Impending doom was right around the corner. I drank more than ever, sometimes first thing in the morning. I was introduced to moonshine and would soon figure out how I could make it at home. I started smoking a lot of cigarettes and stopped giving a fuck about what I ate or how much I drank. I just did whatever I wanted. I was dirty and wet and depressed and things were not going to get better any time soon.

A friend of mine met me in New York—the trail runs just an hour outside of the city. We dropped some acid and went to a concert. He was planning on hiking the rest of the trail with me. After the show, I met a guy selling after-party tickets. I told him that I didn't want one, that I was interested in sleeping pills. He said no problem and returned in 10 minutes with a prescription for Seroquel.

"Forty bucks," he said.

It blew me away. This was a lot easier than that joke of a doctor. They weren't benzos but they would surely put me to sleep for a while. I put them in my pocket and we got in the car and headed back to the trail. We were smoking and listening to music and enjoying the effects of LSD when all of a sudden, red and blue. "Oh shit," I thought, "I can't deal with this right now." There were pills, bottles on the floor, marijuana pipes in the cup holder, and we were high on acid, not to mention two ounces of pot in my backpack. I had completely forgotten about the bottle of pills that were bulging out of my pocket. He pulled us over and you can easily guess what happened. He found the pipes, smelled the weed, found a bunch of pills that weren't prescribed to us. He then searched me and found the bottle of Seroquel, which he thought was an opiate. It was, in fact, unscheduled at the time, so I could not be arrested for possession. He apparently didn't know that and arrested me. I was lucky enough to have Mr. Biggs stay in the holding cell with me until they figured out what to do with me. They let me go. Totally free *and* I still had the rest of my acid and all my pot. Holy shit this was actually really cool, and what a great story!

§

My Life Was Challenging At Prescott (Grayson)

My life was challenging. I made it that way. I didn't know that at the time; it was really fucking hard. I didn't finish the trail. My dog stepped on a porcupine in Massachusetts and that was all I could handle. I had bought some Valium from someone at the library and figured I should quit while I was ahead. I rented a car and drove back to my parents' house to figure out my next move. I was broke and had no plans for the rest of my life. I hadn't completed the trail and there was no magical spiritual experience. I was fucked. I didn't know what I was supposed to do. I was excited to go and visit my friends in Colorado and maybe something would give me direction in my life. I was so lost. I was very lonely.

I went to visit my parents in South Carolina and then drove out to Boulder. The hole inside me was growing at a rapid rate. I just didn't know what I was supposed to do. I needed money, so I tried to start mailing pot from Colorado to South Carolina. I was not able to get the prices I wanted. I thought about going back to school. I would have my parents' support and I knew college kids were the best clients with a steady supply of money from their parents.

I decided to study wilderness leadership at Prescott College. I also planned on growing and selling pot. I had learned a lot from my friends in Colorado and I knew Arizona laws were strict. That meant I could make a lot of money selling pot if I didn't get caught. Growing pot was a great distraction from my pain. It was exciting as was making money and spending it however I wanted.

The first time I grew pot was in an apartment. I do not recommend growing pot in an apartment. Everyone told me it was a bad idea. I made a grow box out of a large dresser and grew four plants in the dresser. If you came over, you would have no idea the dresser was full of lights and plants. I even had a carbon filter inside so it would not smell. I made a few hundred dollars from that grow. More importantly I earned trust from other bigger growers who would give me deals on large quantities to mail back to South Carolina. I didn't want anyone in Arizona knowing the scale of what I was doing, so I tried to keep my clients cross-country. As my finances began to improve, I had bigger and bigger ideas.

During my first year at Prescott, I picked up a needle for the first time. My friend Jack was a heroin addict. He told me that he could get some and I thought all my problems were soon to be solved. For a short while, they were.

The first time I tried heroin, I smoked it. I was not impressed and I knew I wanted to shoot it up. There was no doubt about it. Give it to me the strongest way possible. I had a lot of pain. If you felt like I felt, you would want to shoot it up, too.

The first time I shot up, it was pure heaven. I could feel it all the way to my fingertips. The lights got a little brighter and everything slowed down to a manageable pace. Nothing mattered any more. The hole was filled. All from a tiny piece of black tar heroin that smelled like vinegar. It was cheap, too. I could get a gram for around 60 bucks and it would last me a couple of weeks. I found the missing piece. My long-lost friend. My soul mate. My better half. This was it. School was easier. I could sit through class with no problem. In fact, I looked forward to it.

I excelled in school and this fed my ego, and let me justify shooting up before school. It wasn't long before my good friend, Jack, showed me how to mix a little bit of cocaine with the heroin. That was something else. It was like I became electric for a few seconds. The blood rushing in my head sounded like a train going by. It was loud and I was breathing very hard. It was exhilarating. I could hardly stand it. It was too good to be true. And then it was over. Just like that. Done.

The point is, the heroin kept me from feeling the urge to shoot more cocaine when I crashed. A shot of coke doesn't last very long at all and leaves you wanting more in minutes. Nothing a little bit of heroin can't fix.

One day, I was in the classroom and I had all my supplies with me. I wanted to go to the bathroom to shoot a little speedball. The class was all day and it was very boring. I had a hard time paying attention and I thought that if I shot a little dope, I would retain more critical information. I went to the bathroom and I forgot to lock the door. I was drawing up my magical potion in the rig when someone opened the door. I didn't try to hide it. I didn't even skip a beat. I looked up and made eye contact with the random student. He looked at me and said sorry and closed the door. I went about my business and didn't think twice about it.

Things were getting bad very fast. I was making a lot of money mailing pot back to South Carolina and all of a sudden I needed a gram a day, just for myself. This became tricky because usually Jack and I drove to Phoenix, which was a couple hours away, to pick it up. The prices nearby were twice as much. I got a great idea.

It didn't take me long to realize how much money I could make by buying cheap dope in Phoenix and selling it back in Prescott. In fact, I knew a lot of people who would make it worth my while. So that's what I did. Weekly, I would drive with Jack down to Phoenix and pick up large amounts of heroin and cocaine.

We picked it up from local gangs. Gangbangers had the best, and they were reliable. We never had any trouble. I could hand over 1,000 or 2,000 bucks and they would never give me a short bag. Never. No bullshit. No waiting. No scales and it always weighed out. It was too easy. Every time we went we said we would wait until we got home to shoot it up. We never did.

As soon as we got it, we shot it. Sometimes in plain daylight at a stoplight. It didn't matter if anyone saw. I had to do it. I couldn't stop, but I still didn't know how big a problem I had. Shooting up cocaine and heroin was something I did multiple times a day. I sold lots of pills as well. When I couldn't drive to Phoenix, I had a connection for benzos in Prescott. All the while, I was staying high as a kite and making money. I thought I had arrived and I never had to feel pain again.

I wish it could have stayed like that forever. I had big plans to make $100,000 in a year. I'm not sure if I did or not, because I was always spending my profits on drugs and booze. Lots of it. My personal stash was divided into two bags. One that I could pull out in front of you and one that I didn't want you to know I had, because you would bug me to sell you some. It was all personal. All for me - to keep me afloat.

My second year in school, I had a great plan. I was experimenting with synthesizing DMT. It's a powerful psychedelic drug. It was coined "the spirit molecule" for its ability to leave you with a feeling that you met a deity. I was getting pretty good at making the stuff when I met someone who wanted me to teach him how to do it. I told him I would teach him if he paid for all the precursors (raw materials). We needed to make at least a quarter pound. He threw down around two grand and we got to work. We made all the chemistry equipment from grade-two plastic. I read about being able to do this in a book called *Sources*. It told me everything I needed to know about obtaining equipment for making methamphetamine. We made all the equipment. We bought gallons of different types of solvents including high-grade naphtha, which is used for lighter fluid and needs heating in the process of making DMT. This is the most dangerous part as you could guess. We went through the process in our heads over and over.

We had one shot to make this work and the quicker we did it the less likely we were to get caught manufacturing a Schedule 1 substance. The gravity of what I was doing never sank in. Perhaps because my focus was on all the money I would make. A quarter pound is around 112 grams, each of which I could sell for $150 to $200. Let's take the average $175 x 112 which would make $19,600. Our plans were to take this and make chocolates with 2 pounds of mushrooms and take 2 pounds of weed and go on tour to sell it all at music festivals.

It was a good plan, but we were unable to sell everything in a summer.

We made too much cash too fast. As soon as I got the money, I spent it on drugs. The higher I got, the more I bought because I could. My pockets had cash stuffed in them and I stopped keeping track. It didn't fucking matter. We easily made our money back in a few hours of the first concert.

The morning we were leaving the festival, my friend explained to me that he couldn't keep doing this. I didn't know it at the time, but he was leaving our plan to pursue sobriety. To this day, he is still sober and I hope he can stay that way the rest of his life. We were both drug addicts, but I was not willing to ask anyone for help at the time.

He told me that I could keep all the drugs. He didn't want any. He planned on driving home to Alabama that day to clear his head and get his shit back together. I have never seen anyone eat as many mushrooms as he did the night before. It was very uncomfortable to watch him eat 14 grams of mushrooms. He ate seven 2-gram chocolates. It was baffling that he would ever be able to recover from such an experience. He recovered fully and lives a meaningful and fulfilling life. We are good friends and stay in touch to this day.

So there I was again. Abandoned yet again. Me against the world. I fucking knew it. I would have to do everything. I decided to drive home and sell what I could on the East Coast because the prices were better out there and I had a lot of friends that would want what I had.

My brother was getting into pills and heroin at this time. Or maybe he had been for a long time, but I just began to hear about it turning south for him. I was concerned that my parents were not going to handle it correctly, so I shared my perspective on how he should be treated. How hypocritical of me. Beyond hypocrisy, it's almost lunacy that I thought I knew what was best for him and for his sobriety when I was so fucking lost and broken and alone.

I was driving home with thousands and thousands of dollars worth of drugs intended for distribution when my mother called. She said that my father just had a panic attack after dropping my brother off outside a psych ward. My brother just smoked a few thousand dollars worth of crack and had a mental breakdown. He was in bad shape. It was my first experience with someone in a drug-induced psychosis and he was totally nuts. My father was not handling it well. My mother asked me if I could go pick my father up. I was frozen. I knew that I had to but I didn't want to with all the drugs I had. This was not a good situation. I needed to think about it, but I just couldn't. I just couldn't come to a clear conclusion. Should I throw all the drugs away? We are talking $30,000 worth, at least. This is what I had been working so hard for. It didn't seem fair to me to have to throw them all away. It would crush my father if we got pulled over and he had to witness his eldest son with pounds of numerous drugs get arrested right after dropping his middle child off in a psych ward for a drug-induced psychosis. Shit, I couldn't come up with a clear answer.

Eventually I decided to throw the mushrooms away and keep the rest. I don't know why. It just seemed like the best thing to do. I met my father in Arkansas and we cried. I told him it would all work out and I noticed that if I said positive things like that, it really helped him. It was like this for two days. Any mention of my brother would bring him to tears. So I tried my best to steer the conversation as best I could. I even offered him a marijuana candy to help with anxiety but I'm not sure if he even understood what I was offering.

Somehow we made it home. All the drugs and no more psych ward. I could hardly keep myself together. I was so fucked inside but I couldn't let anyone know. Fortunately, my father had a bottle of my brother's pills. They were Klonopin, which one of my brother's doctors had given him. My brother was abusing them and my father managed to get the pills away from my brother. I told my father I would flush them down the toilet but I pocketed most of them and this is what kept me together for the ride home. The worst was yet to come.

§

I Had No Idea (Patty)

I had no idea at all what Grayson was up to as far as using and selling drugs. At this point, my attention had shifted to his younger brother, Brandon. Grayson had found a school in Arizona that was perfect for him. With his love of the outdoors, he could major in outdoor education. I knew he drank and smoked pot, but had no idea he was making, growing, and selling drugs. We would call on him for advice about Brandon's drug use and how to handle that. I relied on Grayson to help in times of need when his dad could not fly home, calling on Grayson to pick him up. I believed Grayson was in a good place in his life, finally settling on a career path that suited him. He was responsible. I desperately needed that Mary Poppins's way of life to come true. Searching for something to hang onto, I held onto him, my oldest son. It's the best I had at the time. My husband was struggling with Brandon's addiction and my daughter was tired of hearing about our messed up family.

§

Sharing A Needle (Grayson)

I shot up with a borrowed needle just one time. It was early on in my using days. I went from being able to manage my addiction to having no control whatsoever in a matter of weeks. I had forgotten to buy more needles before the pharmacy closed. I went to pick up some stuff from a guy I knew in Prescott. He was a junkie and had been most of his life. He was in his mid 50s and looked decades older. It was a look at my future if I continued down the path I was on. I was sitting in his trailer with a bag of dope. I did not have much and smoking it would have been a waste. I asked around for anyone with a clean rig; no one had one. Most people were smoking it. That was not an option for me. I needed to get this in my bloodstream as pure as I could.

I was sweaty, achy and felt like I was going to throw up. I knew if I shot up some dope everything would be all right again. My friend said he had a used one that I could clean with bleach. This was new to me. I did not know for sure that cleaning it with bleach would work or cause other serious problems. I didn't care too much and I tried not to think about it too much. I followed his instructions and cleaned the syringe with bleach. I was crossing a line and I knew it. Deep down, I knew this was a big deal. This guy had been using since I was born and did not have a healthy or clean lifestyle. He was one of my few using friends that did fit the junkie stereotype and I was going to use one of his rigs. It was worth it to me. I weighed my options. Risk versus reward. I made a decision. I cleaned it out as best as I could. I was excited and my physical and mental body knew relief was coming soon.

Pushing through my thick skin with a dull needle that had been used multiple times by someone else makes me want to puke just thinking about it. I could see the needle bend until it punctured through my thick skin and at first it pushed the vein to the side. I repositioned and broke through. It was not gentle. I could hear the tear as it punctured my vein. It hurt. I didn't care. I was above anything bad happening to me. I was invincible. My blood rushed with the warm comfort of opiates and my eyelids dropped. I could taste the vinegar in the back of my throat. My thought process came to a dead halt. I had peace and serenity for a few hours. I had a few hours to feel alive.

I continued to make compromising decisions around using heroin. I always shot it up. Sometimes I would use the same rig for weeks. At first, it was a new rig every time with sterile water and alcohol swabs. I shot up with used cigarette filters and no filters. Dirty water. Whatever I had to do to get it in my blood, I did. I shot up pills with only using cotton filter and sometimes no filter at all. I pushed a lot of foreign objects into my veins. I lived like this for years and I am grateful that I have no lasting health issues.

Alone And Tired (Grayson)

Alone, tired, bored, dissatisfied, heartbroken and depressed. The list goes on. My life was not satisfactory in any area. Not one single area in my life was working. I lacked adequate social skills. I couldn't keep a job. I did well in school, but it was a struggle and required a lot of assistance like Adderall and cocaine. My life was confusing and exhausting. I was delusional. I kept thinking things would get better even though I continued to drop deeper in the dark hole of addiction. The pain and loneliness I was creating wasn't enough for me to realize there was another way to live. I thought drugs and alcohol were meant for me. I thought they helped me in school. I thought they gave me the social skills I lacked. I thought they made me look better. They fulfilled every single need and desire. I continued to sell drugs. Whatever I could get a deal on, I would try to sell. Mushrooms, marijuana, ecstasy, LSD, Xanax, heroin and cocaine were the most common and easy to sell.

I was living a double life and I was fucking great at it. My school friends hardly knew what was going on. In my later years, they might have known I once had a small problem with heroin or that I experimented with it. But they had no idea. Even more clueless were my parents. They thought I smoked a little pot and they were not happy about that, but the truth would blow their mind. I was doing well in school and that meant a lot to everyone. It took all the energy I had to stitch together all the bullshit and appear to be sober.

I am convinced that the most traumatic thing in my life to this day has been my drug use. Simple using. Not one specific event while I was high. Just being high. Staying up on meth for a couple days is traumatizing. Trying to convince myself I wasn't going to go into cardiac arrest is traumatizing. Passing cops, while driving with illegal substances, made my heart get stuck in my throat and I could feel a prickle in all my veins. That was traumatizing. LSD and mushrooms, well, I don't really need to go into depth there. I took large quantities and started to become more and more paranoid about the people around me. I didn't trust anyone.

Maybe it was the gang activity I was so close to. Maybe it was a lack of sleep. Probably a combination of things, but I needed to have a loaded gun nearby if not right under my mattress. It made me feel safe. I often would have nightmares of people out to get me and I'd wake up in an LSD panic ready to bolt for the door and run. Having a loaded .38 special helped me deal with that.

I met a lot of people in college but failed to form lasting connections. I couldn't be totally vulnerable with anyone. I thought if I opened up to someone they would use that against me later. I had my drugs, my gun, and my money.

I think I did fit in. Somewhat. I went to plenty of parties and had a few girlfriends. I did all the things but at the end of the night there was something that made me different from the rest. Something that only drugs and alcohol could fix. And simply drinking at a party wasn't enough and I knew that. I always had something else. Heroin and/or Xanax were with me everywhere I went. Even on month-long field courses I would make sure I had plenty of Xanax to help me deal with withdrawals and keep me high for weeks. This probably led to some embarrassing situations, most of which I have forgotten - except one.

We were on our wilderness leadership course, the final course before I got my degree. It was winter semester 2013 and we just finished the skiing portion in Idaho. I had some Xanax or Valium, I can't remember. We went to the liquor store after we checked into our hotel and everyone was excited to be back in the front country and around general population. We had a fun time skiing and spirits were high. We all got some booze and were planning on going back to the hotel room to hang out and wash the rest of our gear and clothes. I stopped at a store to get some tincture that would help me sleep. It is called Valerian root and it is quite effective. I didn't know this when I took it, but it helps the human body excrete fluids in the form of urine. I was drinking beer like a fish. I took a couple of pills and instead of using the dropper that the tincture bottle came with, I took a small nip from the bottle. I was out within 30 minutes. I fell asleep with all my clothes on, the TV on, and everyone else still awake and charged with energy.

The next morning I was surprised I slept so long without having to get up to go to the bathroom. Well, I did go to the bathroom, all over the air conditioner unit in the hotel room in front of all my classmates. The evidence was there, a puddle of my urine on the window sill. I don't remember feeling embarrassed at the time. Maybe I did, but I can't tell for sure. I was very good at disconnecting from anything uncomfortable and for this particular incident, that is what I did.

My life was challenging and I was going to be graduating soon. This brought about a lot of anxiety, because I had no plan. I figured I could go see a doctor and tell him that I had IBS, irritable bowel syndrome, and he would more than likely prescribe Xanax. He did just that. I used it all the time. I took all the doctor prescribed and supplemented it with what I bought around town. I had a serious benzo addiction. It turns out that was mild compared to what was about to happen.

My girlfriend at the time believed I had quit using heroin after the summer before my last semester. How I wished that were true. I loved her and we had a real connection. I wanted to be with her the rest of my life and I thought she was the most wonderful person I had ever met. I could breathe when I was around her. For a brief period, she fixed me, but sooner rather than later, the deep, dark depression and sadness settled in. And this time it was hard to hide. It was hard to hide from someone I loved so much. I didn't want her to see how I felt. She wouldn't like me if she saw that.

I got back into heroin, but tried to keep it under control. This caused my benzo use to be out of control. It doesn't really matter what drug I was using. I was after the same effect; to appear like a whole and happy person to the one I loved so she would want to be with me the rest of her life. That's twisted and sick and I knew it. She couldn't fix me. I couldn't fix me. The drugs helped briefly. For some odd fucking reason that didn't make a lot of sense to me. My girlfriend and I moved to Oregon and lived together out of a car. No more heroin. I could no longer drive to Phoenix and pick it up. But I still had my prescription of Xanax and began to drink more. Anytime I stopped one drug, I used another one a lot more.

I don't think being in love really helped. When I felt a real emotion, I was quick to cover it up. I didn't know where I was going and now someone else was twisted up in my story. I needed to quit before she figured me out, but I didn't feel happy without drugs. I was sure she would leave me if I wasn't happy.

We did all sorts of once-in-a-lifetime adventures. Benzos kept me away from heroin and satisfied enough to be able to do those things. We worked at a wilderness therapy place together and hated it. The cool part was being able to mountain bike for eight days during our off shift. I still wanted to grow pot and felt I was wasting my time making so little money doing something I hated.

Our relationship had serious problems right from the beginning. Co-dependency was strong. Life was more confusing. I just wanted to get drunk and sometimes go on a bike ride. She wanted to exercise for 10 hours and skip most meals. I wanted to go out to eat and out again for dessert. It was a wreck. Similar to my relationship with drugs and alcohol, I held onto her as long as I could. I was certain she was my soul mate because no one else could possibly love me. I thought it was a miracle that I found someone who did. It wasn't much of a miracle. It was one of the most painful experiences in my short life, and it didn't get better. Nothing did.

She began to express her concern that I was drinking too much and my reply was usually something along the lines of "at least I'm not doing heroin," which was true, because at that time I wasn't. But I wanted to. Very badly. I also wanted to get off the benzos, but I could not afford to even try that. I continued to drink in pursuit of the effects produced by heroin. This led me to be very irritable and unhappy with everything and everyone.

I was terrified. I couldn't make decisions and I hated myself. I would drink early in the day, fall asleep early in the evening ,and wake up in a panic in the dark hours of the morning. I felt so alone. A lot of times the best way to deal with it was to take a few shots and a Xanax. It was all I knew.

My life was becoming unmanageable. The hardest times were when my girlfriend was working and I was just hanging out waiting for her to get off. I had no distractions for the day and I would camp by myself in the woods. I had no friends in Oregon outside of work. At the latest, I would start drinking at noon. It was a struggle to stay awake until 5:00. I would watch TED Talks on my phone or go into town and use the wifi at a McDonalds or a coffee shop. I was desperate to make friends and I thought I was giving it a good shot, but really I was drowning myself. I was suffocating.

I really wanted to ski and as the winter approached, I told my girlfriend I wanted to live somewhere I could ski everyday. I thought it would help with the pain and depression and maybe I could stop taking so many pills. How did I let this happen again? Why can't I control the amount of pills I take?

She had just finished with a backpacking trip in Mammoth Lakes, California. It was winter of 2014 and I was a wreck, but I was excited to ski. The plan was to meet her in Mammoth Lakes and climb in the Sierras for a week or so before trying to figure out the rest of our lives. We met up after the trip and Mammoth was beautiful. It was small with only a couple of stoplights and huge mountains. Mammoth is notorious for huge winter storms and deep snow. I was excited again. She had some friends in the area and they were looking for roommates. We met another fellow who worked at a rental shop and assured us he could get us jobs and a ski pass. That was all I needed to hear. I was sold. I love skiing more than anything else. I was convinced that if I could ski every day, I wouldn't have to drink so much or take so many pills.

§

If She Dies, She Dies (Patty)

My life is and has been a bit overwhelming. I have lived around several addicts for many years. When Grayson left for Colorado, I felt relieved and hopeful, thinking the geographical change would do some good. Out of sight and out of mind helped relieve some of my anxiety. And my concern for Grayson switched to my other son, Brandon. Brandon was in and out of rehab and detox. I became more consumed with his addiction and recovery. Feeling sick to my stomach and unable to catch my breath were physical side effects of my life. Prayer and relying on my recovery community kept me afloat. Desperately crying out for help was an everyday practice.

I went to see the movie, *Exotic Marigold Hotel,* and heard a line from the movie, "If she dies, she dies," humorously referring to the frailty and old age of a character in the movie. I quickly adopted this phrase for the characters in my life. Finding myself in situations where I had no control, I would quote this line in my head, "If she dies, she dies," and let go of any worry or illusion of control I might have over someone else. I cannot add or take away a single day of someone's life. My sons' lives in their active addiction or attempts of recovery were out of my hands. It was not my job, even as their mom, to cure them. I was then able to "let go and let God," "live and let live," and take life "one day at a time."

They would often call me in moments of need and I learned to respond, "I know you know what to do. I know you'll figure it out." I could empower them to take responsibility for themselves.

§

Sitting In The Pain (Patty)

I have learned to sit in the pain. My tendency was to run far away from the pain. When my life brought times of heartache or trauma, I first turned to chocolate. It was readily available and most effective in numbing my pain. I also had dreams in my head to drive out of town, up I-26, and keep on going. In recovery, I have learned to deal with pain, disappointment, and heartache by facing it and feeling the feelings. I treat my pain with great intentionality, recognizing my uncomfortable feelings and accepting them. Walking and praying help me process what's going on. I also stop, sit, and let the feelings wash over me.

I have learned to grieve better. Grieving is a gift that helps me heal. When I accept the challenges I have had, I can function in a healthier way and things don't come out sideways. I can live a more centered life, free from worry and fear.

§

Finding Heroin In Mammoth (Grayson)

My girlfriend and I moved into a house with three people. I told everyone that I wanted to ski and grow pot. Everyone in the house was ok with that. I had grown 99 plants in Arizona and it was one of the most stressful and profitable decisions of my life. Making that kind of cash is hard to walk away from. I was eager to do it again. Plus, I still had all the equipment I needed. If I could just ski and grow pot, I would be all right.

I could not stick to my plan. It didn't take long for me to find out where to get heroin and cocaine. I was working in a ski rental shop and I hated it. I made $9.80 an hour and I was a college graduate. I felt like a joke. This was the least amount of money I had ever made in my entire life. I got drunk every day and sometimes during work hours.

One day someone walked into the rental shop in the afternoon when we were pretty slow. He smelled like he had been carrying a dead skunk around for days. That was one of my favorite smells. I commented on it. Something along the lines of "man you got something that smells really good". He told me that he had some incredible pot. He asked me if I wanted to come up to his room to smoke some. His room was part of the hotel where the ski shop was that I was working in. I put a sign on the wall: "Back in 10 minutes." We walked right past the front desk and up the stairs in the lobby. Everyone could see what I was doing, but I thought that it was so obvious they would never suspect anything. I was right.

We got stoned and talked skiing. He lived in LA and had come to Mammoth to ski with his soon-to-be-divorced wife and his newborn baby. He was fishing for a place to stay so he didn't have to pay for hotels when he came to visit. He was turning out to be a real douche bag. That didn't bother me too much because I was using him for his pot and I was certain he could get harder stuff if he lived in LA. Boy was I right.

The next time he came to visit he stayed at our house and was a horrible houseguest with a baby. He and his wife were ungrateful and did not participate in the house dinners and bullshit sessions. I didn't give a flying fuck because he brought up a couple ounces of cocaine and a couple ounces of Molly (what kids call Ecstasy these days). Now I had a plan to make some money this winter. This stuff was as good as gold in a small ski town that parties all day everyday. I easily sold grams of each for 100 bucks. The only problem was that I didn't have anything that would help me come down off the coke. This was easily solved. Having that much of a sought-after substance makes it really easy to find other drugs, as people are eager to trade and barter. I found a solid heroin connection from one of the bellhops at the hotel and it was back to the races.

I was making a couple hundred dollars a day and using a couple hundred dollars of cocaine and heroin a day. I didn't stand a chance to live a sober life. I knew I had a problem but told myself it was a good problem. I was going to be a drug addict for the rest of my life. I figured if I came to accept this, it would make everything a lot easier. I rationalized my lifestyle by never sharing needles and taking breaks from shooting dope. I never shared needles but I would use the same one for weeks. I was an emotional wreck. I also really wanted to get on ski patrol, and with the help of heroin and cocaine, I was able to drink and smoke less, therefore making it more likely for me to make it on ski patrol.

I did make it on ski patrol and my feeling of inferiority reared its ugly head more then ever. I told myself I was fat and slow. I was the worst skier and someone made a mistake to hire me. I constantly made mistakes and punished myself for every little mistake. I thought if I were hard on myself I would become a better person. That is not what happened. I met another guy who was friends with the guy who brought me cocaine. My new friend could get prescription painkillers whenever I wanted and as many as I wanted. It was insane. I could show up in LA with 2 grand and he would have no problem with my request.

I began to shoot up roxys or blues as they are sometimes called - 30 mg of Oxycontin. The problem was I could never get enough in the syringe. It was a task to crush up three of them with enough water and get all the medicine in the rig. This was my life. It was how I operated. I took rigs that were ready to go with me on ski patrol. I took cocaine on tin foil ready to be smoked. And I always had a bag of Xanax in my chest pocket to deal with the horrible come down of it all. My life was hard and it was unclear to me that it was all my own doing. I blamed it on outside circumstances: the weather, my upbringing, and my bosses' poor communication skills.

When ski patrol was over I worked for a school in Santa Monica. They have a great Outdoor Education program and I made decent money. The best part about this job was I could get to LA a day before and pick up whatever drugs I would need for the next two weeks of working in the field. I told my girlfriend that I needed pills to sleep and she seemed to be ok with that. The truth was I needed pills and heroin to sleep and cocaine to wake up. I spent most of my time in the field, high as a kite, while supervising high school kids. I always wore sunglasses and some of the kids thought that was strange. It was strange. I was in a strange place.

Car Camping (Grayson)

I lied a lot. It started with one and led to many more. It wasn't just my guilty conscience that was stressful; it was the fear of getting caught in my lies, specifically by the girl I was dating. I was infatuated with her and didn't want her to find out who I really was, because I was afraid she would leave me. I sold my car for 6K and used the money to buy a couple ounces of cocaine and a couple ounces of Molly. It wasn't my plan to sell the car and buy drugs, it just worked out like that. I couldn't handle saving that type of cash when I saw a good investment. It was the best cocaine I had ever seen in my life- and a lot of it. I had a problem with heroin and not cocaine, I reasoned with myself. I would be able to sell it for $100 a gram in the small ski town I lived in. Everyone wanted it. Especially my manager at the ski shop where I worked. I would take 3 to 4 grams with me to work and sell a couple and do a couple. We used a ski in the back for snorting lines. It was exhausting to do cocaine all day long. I was still turning a profit, but not nearly as much as I had hoped. For every gram I sold, I would do one or maybe two.

One day, I went to a friend's house to sell him a gram, and he was blown away at the quality. He was excited, because he said he would be able to get a good rush from smoking it off tin foil. He showed me how to do it. That experience changed my relationship with cocaine for the rest of my life. I would never waste it up my nose again. I was going to smoke it or shoot it up. Smoking it was nice, because it was almost as strong and didn't leave a track mark. A night of shooting up cocaine leaves a lot of bruises and track marks. After he showed me how to smoke it, I went off the deep end.

All I wanted was to feel that rush. I would lock myself in the bathroom all night long with a roll of tin foil and baking soda. My plan was always the same - to go in for a hit or two. I would stay in there all night long. Sometimes I would come to on the floor with no idea how long I was out and the only thing I was concerned about was getting more cocaine on the tin foil for another hit. I ate very little. I would try not to do it at work. I would hold out as long as I could because I knew once I started, I would be going to the bathroom or the back of the shop every few minutes.

I took some needles with me to work so I could shoot up and avoid the smell of smoke. It was unsatisfying and frustrating, because I had to go back to work at some point and all I wanted was that rush. I did this for about three weeks-smoking and shooting up cocaine. I would do heroin at night to come down. I would also get in bed and take the biggest shot I thought I could handle, so when I crashed, I could just lie in bed and go to sleep. My theory was the bigger the rush, the bigger the crash, and I was more likely to pass out afterwards. My roommates were suspicious and my girlfriend was gone for a month working. She had no clue until she saw me. Apparently, it was obvious that I had been smoking and shooting up cocaine all month. She was shocked, horrified and confused. I told her I was sick. She wanted to believe me.

We went bowling with some friends and I was almost out of cocaine but I had plenty of heroin. I got really high. All the lights were bright and I was irritable from cocaine withdrawals. I made it known that I hated bowling and I did not want to be there. I went to the bathroom to do another shot. When I came back, my girlfriend was hysterical. My friend that I bought heroin from told her what I had been doing. What an asshole, I thought. It was all his fault. He promised he wouldn't say anything. The only thing I blamed myself for was being honest with my friend. He was the one that caused all this, not me. I was delusional and hurt. He betrayed me and now my girlfriend was mad at me. I jumped into the victim role as quickly as I could. I cried and told her how horrible I felt and how sick I was. I was desperate for some sympathy and I got some.

She didn't trust me after that, but she felt bad for me and told me she wasn't going to leave me. Somehow, she found the rest of my cocaine and my reaction was to be pissed off, but I couldn't let her see that. I was going to be sober from hard drugs for her.

She told me she never wanted me to do cocaine again. I said that was not reasonable, but that I wouldn't shoot it up anymore. That was a lie. Everything was a lie.

It wasn't working out living with our roommates, so my girlfriend and I decided to live out of our car and camp at a nearby campground. This allowed me to isolate like never before. She would go work for a couple weeks out of town, and it was just me and my needles in the woods. I was sick in every sense of the meaning. I was alone. I was terrified. All I wanted to do was sleep and I couldn't sleep all day, so I got high. I didn't have any more cocaine left because I couldn't afford it, but I still had shitloads of Molly. I didn't know what would happen if I shot that up, but I was going to find out. It is hard to explain. It certainly felt good, but it left me clenching my jaw and breathing hard. I would sweat immediately and after a few minutes the rush was over and I felt sick and irritable.

Afterwards, my body felt drained. The only thing that made sense was to do another shot. Gram after gram, I would shoot up Molly. I kept saying this shot is going to be my last but I kept doing it. I was insane. The only way to stop was to get as drunk as possible in hopes I would forget about it.

Countless times I would do my "last shot" and then bury my needles in the woods only to dig them up minutes later and pick up exactly where I left off. I could not stop. I wanted to stop more than anything. It seemed impossible. I had a problem for sure and I was convinced that drug addicts like me don't get sober. It was in my DNA to shoot up drugs the rest of my life. My tolerance for emotional pain and self-hate was through the roof. I proved to myself time and time again that I was trash. My life amounted to nothing. I was condemned to live a tortuous life, always trying to fix how I felt with a substance. If you told me that I could have anything that resembled peace and serenity, I would not pay you any attention because that was crazy. If you said anything like that, it just proved that you didn't know me or what you were talking about.

§

Feeling Misunderstood (Patty)

I remember a dark time in my life when I felt all alone. We were having neighbor problems. We had lived in six places before and never once had issues with our neighbors. But now we did. We had friends on the other side of the neighborhood, but those who lived closest to us had "issues" with us. I felt isolated and misunderstood. Many times during the three years living there I was verbally accosted. My kids were shunned and accused of things they were not guilty of.

Often the opposite was true, the kids of the accusers were guilty of what my kids were being accused of. Several of the people living nearby were "holier than thou" and critical. I had several friends tell me I should move to the other side of our neighborhood, away from the critics. I felt so alone and misunderstood.

One evening stands out. I was home alone and having a conversation with my neighbor. After I hung up, I realized I had just been insulted and attacked. The irony was overwhelming. Alone I sat, not able to reach my husband. I began reflecting on Jesus and His life on earth, how He was the most misunderstood being I could think of. I knew He understood my pain and aloneness. I felt comforted and validated. Being understood is vital to my well-being and at this particular moment I found hope in God when no one else was around.

I also have a knack for taking things personally. Thankfully, now, I am able to separate myself from the situation and recognize it's just the other person's opinion. Often it's their "stuff" and has nothing to do with me. How liberating it's been for me to "live and let live" and put principles above personalities.

§

Voice (Patty)

When I was young, I owned a cassette player/recorder. That black box provided hours of entertainment. Olivia Newton John and Amy Grant were my favorite artists. I loved Newton John's "Have You Never Been Mellow" and Grants's "El Shaddai." I have always liked smooth, melancholy music.

I also discovered the world of recording. I recorded hit songs off the radio and my own voice onto blank cassettes. Wow, is that really what I sound like? I worked on improving my speaking voice over and over the recorded message. Also, looking back to when I was young, I see I did not use my voice. I seldom spoke up for myself. I was the "baby" in the family and was directed by my older brothers and parents as to what to do. I held these authority figures in my life in high regard, and I desperately wanted to please them and do as I was told. An underlying fear accompanied my desire to keep them happy. When I married I applied the same pressure to myself, and put my husband's needs above my own, at the expense of losing myself.

Finding my voice came many years later. Seeing that I can and should have a voice shocked me. I can actually be an adult and not live in fear of those around me whom I've given a position of authority. No longer do I need to give others' opinions power over my life. The weight is lifted and I have a voice. I now own my opinions, desires, hopes and dreams. Learning to be true to myself.

§

Manuel (Grayson)

Movies like *Scarface* and rappers that talked about all the money they made from selling drugs inspired me. I was infatuated. I wanted that. I liked the part about how they didn't need anyone. I liked the idea that I could make a lot of money on my own. I wanted so badly to be self-supporting through dealing drugs. For a short time, I was making a good profit from selling drugs to college students. After that, I only thought I was.

I met a guy who was a club promoter in LA who sold me cocaine and Molly. He introduced me to his friend who sold prescription pills. His name was Manuel and he was fascinating. He always wore suits. He always pulled up in a different luxury car than the one before. In my mind he was killing it. He was making the type of money I wanted to be making.

I would call him up and ask him for 100 Roxys, 100 Klonopin, and 200 Valium and he would ask me when. If I said 30 minutes, he'd say no problem. How could he get all those pills to me in such a short time?

I fantasized about his lifestyle. Maybe he had mob connections. I wanted to be a part of organized crime. Manuel was always flying out of the country. He went to all the popular shows in LA. He didn't seem to have a drug problem. He had nice clothes and jewelry. I was amazed at his lifestyle. He was nice, too. He would remember our conversation from the previous week and ask how I had been. I wanted to be Manuel. I thought I was. I was not.

I would spend all the cash I had on pills, and take them back to my dark apartment in Mammoth Lakes to shoot them up. I had plans to sell them and make money, but it never worked out. I drove a shitty Kia Optima that I split with my girlfriend for $1,800. I wore dirty clothes and couldn't afford a haircut. I was addicted and I was abrasive. I was nothing like Manuel. He never called me to try and sell me anything. I always contacted him first. I could trust him. I could send him money in the mail and he would overnight the pills. I had a connection all my friends envied. I still couldn't use it to turn a profit. He sold me the pills dirt-cheap and I could sell them for three or four times as much as I bought them but I only sold enough to be able to buy more and would do the rest. It was frustrating. I tried so hard to be like him. As hard as I tried, I could not pull it off. I was losing money. I was losing my mind

§

Visiting South Carolina For A Month (Grayson)

The next few years in Mammoth were some of the hardest years of my life. If you asked me during that time, I would have convinced you otherwise. I got a job at ski patrol, which I thought would fix my loneliness. Instead it multiplied my feelings of inadequacy. I thought I was dating the girl of my dreams. Over time, it turned into a horrible, unfulfilling relationship that left me full of jealousy and even more feelings of inadequacy. I started going to therapy and my problems got worse, because I wasn't able to be honest. I lied to myself everyday. I lied to countless others. I was selling pot, but it was hard to sell enough to support my 100 dollars a day or more drug habit. I had no real friends.

During this time at Mammoth I would lose all of what little I had. It hurt to lose it all. Within a matter of weeks my dog died, my girlfriend left me, I totaled our car, got kicked out of housing, and lost my ski patrol job and all outdoor Ed contracts for the summer. I was totally broken with nowhere to go, right around my birthday. The heartache was so intense it was physical. I was suffocating—the only way to breathe was to use heroin.

Around this time, one of my therapists suggested it might be a good idea for me to check out Alcoholics Anonymous. He also gave me the Big Book of Alcoholics Anonymous. I was excited and nervous. I was excited to try something new and I was nervous it wouldn't work. I got home and opened the book. I was angry to see the word " God" everywhere. Then I felt stupid. Of course there was a catch. It was a religious thing my therapist wanted me to join. I closed the book and gave it back to him the following week.

I had further to go before I would reach rock bottom. I was desperate to quit drinking and using. I thought I wanted to marry the girl I was dating. I thought if I went home to South Carolina for a month and rode my bike and rested a lot, I would get sober. The hard part was going to be getting off all the pills. Once I wasn't dependent on them anymore, it would be a breeze. I just wouldn't take anymore.

I needed some cash to fund my trip, so I bought a couple thousand dollars' worth of 30 mg Oxycontin to sell in South Carolina. I ended up doing all of them in a couple short weeks. During my month-long stay at home, I shot up more cocaine and slammed more pills than any time in my life. How was this possible? My intentions were strong. My addiction was a lot stronger. I was strung out.

When it was time to go back to Mammoth, I bought 300 Xanax bars to sell when I got back. I was also taking at least five to maintain myself as a functional human. I was on everything. At one point in my life, Xanax helped me withdraw. Cocaine gave me energy just when I needed it. Heroin helped me sleep, so did booze. Now I needed all these things around the clock and it was a nightmare. I felt like I couldn't get high. I was just insane. I was physically addicted to everything in amounts that were scary to me.

I kept a notebook to try to keep up with how many pills I took and when I drank in an effort to help wean me off substances. This didn't work for a second. I would look at my notepad in disbelief and take more Xanax, and shoot more cocaine. It gave me brief periods of relief. During this time I got really sick and got an infection in my arm. I had a fever and almost no energy. I had made plans with my girlfriend to go on a climbing trip when I got home.

I knew I was in trouble, but still didn't know how much it was going to suck to come off all these substances. I ordered some anabolic steroids to be delivered to California when I got there. That was my genius plan: steroids to help with withdrawals. I could hardly walk up a flight of stairs without fainting. Somehow, I got through security with over 60 needles in my carry-on, which I must have overlooked. I was sick as a dog. A lady asked me if I would switch seats with her because I had the aisle. I didn't say anything. I just looked at her and she got the picture. I wasn't moving unless I had to shit or throw up. Which would be about every twenty minutes of the five-hour flight to LA.

I fantasized about how wonderful it would be if it crashed and I died. I was too afraid to ever kill myself. Yet, I couldn't stop thinking about how all my problems would be solved if the plane had just crashed. That didn't happen. I had a friend meet me in Mammoth Lakes airport to drive me back to my place. I had my 300 Xanax bars, but they did very little to sooth the withdrawals from cocaine, opiates and booze. I was too tired to pursue more drugs and too scared to see the withdrawals through. As awful as this experience was, my life would still get worse before I made a decision to turn things around.

I was sick as a dog and I had a large infection on my arm from an injection site. It was painful to bend my elbow and I could not disguise it with makeup. I told my girlfriend it was an infected mosquito bite I got from working in my parents' garden. She chose to believe me.

I waited a couple days until I was in too much pain to handle and I went to the emergency room. I attempted the same lie, but they didn't buy it. I told them the truth. The hospital was very small and I worked with a lot of the hospital employees because of ski patrol. I didn't want them to know why I was there. I would end up in the hospital a lot the next few months and everyone slowly got the idea. They cut me open and drained all the pus, stitched me back up, and sent me on my way with some antibiotics. I kept telling my girlfriend it was a mosquito bite. I could not sleep at night, I felt so guilty. I was so ashamed and I knew I had to tell her the truth. It was just a matter of time.

I went to my first AA meeting when I got out of the hospital and the atmosphere blew me away. Everyone was smiling and laughing. Except for me, of course. I didn't stop crying for two weeks. Every time I tried to share about my life it brought me to tears. My life was dreadful and shameful. I was going to meetings because I didn't want my girlfriend to leave me, and I thought it would prove to her that I was willing to do whatever to stop. I still knew that drugs and alcohol would provide instant relief from my misery.

I stayed sober for a couple weeks until I'd decide to pick up a couple beers on my way home and the relief was instant. I could get some sleep and I even felt better the next day. Unfortunately, this behavior led to many more rock bottoms before I was so desperate I was willing to do anything it took, but that would be more than a year later.

This time of my life was terrible. I wanted to stay sober in the meetings and as soon as I left I needed a beer or some heroin. I couldn't make it to the next meeting without getting high. Eventually I would get high and go to meetings. I wanted what the people in the meetings had. I related to them. They used drugs and alcohol like I did and they found a way out. I did not have enough pain to convince me that my plans were not working and I kept on trying.

I gave up the idea of being sober, but somehow found it necessary to lie to my family and friends about it. My girlfriend left me and immediately got in a relationship with someone else. That was my excuse to pick up the needle again and again. Every time I thought about her or him I would get drunk or high and that was a lot.

§

Any Lengths (Patty)

When my oldest was two, we would read books all the time. Reading on a little blue love seat, snuggled together, were cherished moments. One of his favorite characters was Curious George. The little, mischievous monkey going on countless adventures intrigued my little one. So, I set out to find a "real" Curious George stuffed monkey. There were counterfeit ones around, but I had to find the real one. Dad joined in the search and we called around town. Finally locating Curious George at a toy store in downtown Atlanta, hopping in the car, toddler buckled in, we headed downtown. I was willing to go to any lengths to obtain the little furry friend. What a joy for me to hand the cute stuffed animal to my little boy. Sharing this moment with my dad created a special memory with him, who, when I was growing up, taught me there is usually a way to accomplish any task. I would go to any lengths to achieve what I was passionate about.

Today I am passionate about my health and well being, and I will go to any lengths to live freely. Like Dad teaming up with me to find the monkey, I surround myself with people who support and encourage me. I am searching for real, genuine recovery and committed to the journey.

§

Last Car Wreck (Grayson)

I have been in too many car wrecks to count, in which three, the car rolled over. They were all drug and alcohol related. I have had two DUIs and escaped countless others. It is a wonder that no one was ever seriously injured or killed. The last car wreck I was in was the most humiliating on many different levels. I was living in Mammoth Lakes at the time and I was on ski patrol. This was a job I had wanted for years and worked hard to get. I was raised in South Carolina, and there is no skiing there. I learned to ski when I was 22-years-old and a lot of the other ski patrol had been skiing their entire lives. It was a challenging job to get and it proved too challenging for me to keep while I was drinking and using.

Around this time I had started going to my first AA meetings and attempting sobriety. At the time, I thought I was willing to go to any length to achieve sobriety, but I hardly knew what this meant. I had detoxed from benzos and heroin and alcohol. I was starting to feel clearheaded. I was also extremely lonely. I didn't have any friends in town that didn't drink or use and I hadn't made any friends in the program yet. I was bored and sitting with my pain when I decided to give an old friend a call just to see what he was up to. He invited me over to his house. I didn't even like hanging out with the guy, but I was so desperate that it sounded fun. It was better than sitting alone in my misery.

I went over to his house around four in the afternoon and he offered me a beer. I declined, but quickly changed my answer. Nothing bad will happen if I just drink beer. I had another. Then we started to drink whiskey. Then he found a connection for Xanax, then for hydrocodone. I had no tolerance anymore, yet I picked up exactly where I left off. I took two Xanax bars and a handful of hydrocodone. Then I remembered I had a handful of empty bags of Molly I could scrape and snort.

I left his house and went to snort some Molly alone. I was back at it in full force, with whatever substance I could take to mask the feelings of guilt and shame. The people in the rooms of Alcoholics Anonymous call this the phenomena of craving. Once I take that first sip or first hit, I can't get enough. I was desperate to cover up how I felt. It was painful and I didn't know how to make it go away without pills and booze and weed.

Over the years, there are long periods I don't remember because of all the benzos. I lost a few hours that night and the Molly gave me enough energy to drive around town by myself. I have no recollection of what I was doing from about midnight to 5 a.m. There was nothing like a good car wreck to sober me up. I was driving down Main Street with not a single car on the road and no obstacles to hit. I was going about 35 mph according to the police report. I hit the curb and rolled the car over in front of a parked police car. I was startled. Glass was everywhere. I felt nothing. I was floating in space. I could taste the familiar metallic taste of blood as I was sitting upside down being held by the seat belt. Within minutes, rude blinding lights where in my face. I knew I was caught. I was totally honest with the police. Yes, I had been drinking. No, I don't want to do sobriety test and waste everyone's time. Just arrest me.

Drool and blood were leaking out of my lip that I bit through. They searched the car. I had absolutely no idea what they were going to find. Had I picked up more drugs? It was all over and I didn't care. They found an empty bottle of whiskey, Jim Beam, my favorite, and asked me whose it was. I had absolutely no idea who was riding in my backseat drinking whiskey out of the bottle.

I got arrested for a DUI and questioned about someone breaking into a vehicle. I would never do anything like that, I explained. And then a sliver of memory came back. It was me. I had broken into someone's car looking for God knows what when someone came out to go to work and caught me red handed with latex gloves on my hands. Where the hell did I get latex gloves? This was humiliating in such a small town.

Apparently, I told the owner of the vehicle my first and last name and address. At least I was honest. He didn't press charges and I didn't take anything out of his car. The police asked if I wanted to go to the hospital. Painkillers, I thought. At least something good would come out of this.

The ambulance arrived and what happened next was probably the most humiliating experience. I knew I looked rough. I had blood on my white shirt and I had ingested a lot of different substances. I was past the part of the high where I feel like I look good. I felt like a dirty homeless crackhead and I was sure that's what I looked like. The first responder was the assistant director of ski patrol. I was shocked. He didn't acknowledge who I was; he just asked me what was I thinking.

I didn't say anything as I lay on the backboard in the back of the ambulance. I just looked into his eyes. I couldn't believe my actions. I was fucking up everything faster than ever. Could I get fired for this? I was pretty sure he couldn't say anything because of the confidentiality laws but this was a small town.

They took me to the hospital and the sun was starting to come up and I was starting to realize how big of a deal this was. I was going to lose ski patrol and my summer contracts working Outdoor Ed because I wouldn't be able to drive a company vehicle. My girlfriend was probably going to leave me. The car was totaled. This was overwhelming and much too similar to the first car accident I was in when I was 15. Had I learned anything in the last 10 years?

I was stuck in shitty circumstances. Nothing had gone my way, I couldn't catch a break and it was exhausting. My friend picked me up from the hospital and took me home. I just wanted to go to sleep and hope something would resolve itself when I woke up. I had a long list of things to do and people to tell what just happened, and I dreaded it. The fact that I was a piece of shit drug addict was becoming all too clear for me to handle. I was a disappointment to everyone and no one could count on me. I felt worthless. I lay on the floor of my dark dingy apartment and tried to put all the pieces together. It was too messy to make any sense of it, but I kept trying. I kept analyzing and dissecting my life to figure out what went wrong. I couldn't sleep and I couldn't come up with a satisfactory answer to anything. My heart hurt and I had no one and nothing to help with the pain. Alone again.

§

Years Later (Patty)

Several years passed and I finally began to pay more attention to my own journey of recovery. More traumas came up in our family and I developed more of a plan to take care of myself. I had lost myself and needed to make myself a priority.

I began meeting with a therapist who offered a six-month therapy group for co-addicts that would meet every week for two hours. Explaining the requirements and monetary cost, she asked if I could afford the group. "I can't afford not to," I replied.

I worked really hard doing all of the assignments and better understanding addiction. The final section of the group was all about developing a recovery plan. I would come up with ways to better care for myself in all areas of my life—physical, emotional, and spiritual. I was finding my voice and myself. It was so empowering and liberating.

I embraced the concept of surrender and community and became involved in my own 12-step groups. I got a sponsor and worked the steps.

Much was revealed to me as I continued down my path of recovery. I was able to let go of others' recovery and focus on my own. Respecting others struggle became second nature. "Live and let live" revolutionized my standard way of operating. I no longer had to save my family (or the world). I could breathe. Letting those around me take responsibility for their own lives, I was free to live mine.

§

Self Care (Patty)

I have recently learned what it means to take care of myself. Through extensive therapy I learned the importance of self care and that I can't give what I don't have. For years I gave and gave until there was very little left of me. Self-care is not selfish. It's critical. I can now give more freely and from a healthier place.

Several years ago I came up with a self-care plan: what it looks like emotionally, physically and spiritually to take care of myself. I took each area of my life and laid out a plan, actions to do everyday. Defining what I need was the first step. This self-actualization helped me to see specifically what I needed for personal health and growth. Getting enough sleep, learning to relax and breathe, laughing and smiling are a few areas I reviewed. Eating good food and getting exercise are important ways I care for myself. I have identified unhealthy coping and replaced with healthy coping. I have developed hobbies and other ways to have fun. I pursue a spiritual practice and connection with God through prayer and meditation. I treat myself kindly and avoid self-criticism. I also journal and reach out for support.

I lead with "yes" when invited to join in an activity, and am not afraid to say "no" when I need to. I have choices and opportunities to live a life of purpose. I'm valuable and important and I am glad I have learned ways to care for myself.

§

Confidential Informant (Grayson)

I started working at a nearby restaurant serving food. I hate the food and beverage industry, but it allowed me to use regularly. I pretty much stopped selling pot by this time, because I couldn't afford it financially. My credit card debt was growing and I wanted to die. I would try to get exercise occasionally, because I knew it would help with depression. I loved being outside. It was hard for me to get out unless I was high on heroin. One day I got a bag of dope and decided to go on a hike. It was peaceful and quiet. It was the best time I had had in a long time. I was exhausted from life but not during that hike. It was a combination of the heroin and being outside that made me feel ok for once.

I got back to my apartment and was about to hop in the shower, when all of a sudden three undercover police came swarming in and immediately arrested me. I was shocked. I hadn't sold any pot for at least six months and I wasn't doing anything else illegal. The amounts of heroin I were buying were not a big deal. I couldn't figure it out. Then one of the agents pulled down his face-mask and said, "Do you remember me?"

"Motherfucker," I thought. I sure did. He was the last person I sold hash to. It was very inconvenient for me and I only sold him a couple grams. I didn't like selling such small amounts and that is why it was easy to remember the experience.

When I first moved to California, I was involved in manufacturing large amounts of hash from my friends' trimmings. Most people were usually sick of it and didn't know what to do with 55-gallon bags full of this stinky stuff, and that is when I would make my proposal. "I'll process all of it into some top-shelf hash in a matter of days and split the yield."

People loved it and I ended up with pounds of free hash. The police must have known I was doing this, which is why they didn't arrest me immediately when I sold an undercover agent the hash. They wanted to open an investigation on me and catch me in the act or set me up to sell a couple pounds. Lucky for me, I was too sick into my addiction to keep doing that. I just gave it up and focused more on acquiring heroin for personal use, which the police also figured out after following me around for six months. I had the feeling that I was being followed or watched as most people do when they are strung out on drugs. To find out it was true, sent my paranoia to a whole new level.

They knew I was a junky and they intended to use that against me. Initially, I didn't think it was a big deal that I sold someone a couple grams of hash. After all, this was California, weed is legal here, right? I was wrong. It was a felony punishable with three years in prison. That is a large chunk of my life. More than that I would be a felon for the rest of my life. No more owning a firearm. No more student loans for school. It would be very limiting for the rest of my life. The severity was beginning to sink in. They offered me a plea bargain that would reduce my sentence to 18 months of drug court, but I would have to rat on someone bigger than me. Furthermore, I would have to set them up three times.

The police were ready with the perfect candidates as they had a good idea who I was buying dope from. My first thought was to just take the charges. It seemed like the most straightforward option. Plus, I could probably score dope in prison, no big deal. I told the police I needed to think about it, and they gave me one day to give them an answer. My instructions were to tell no one and call them back when I had an answer. I got home and called a lawyer. This was a bad idea. In doing so, it communicated to the police that I was getting ready to take the charges, which they would file against me.

After talking to a lawyer, I called someone from the program who I had been most honest with about my life. I told him what I did and what my options were. He told me that I should just take the charges because I would probably be a junky the rest of my life and this way I wouldn't get killed. He said if I decided to be a confidential informant and keep using, I would probably end up dead sooner than later. He said prison is not that big of a deal and that he had done six years. He went on to explain that if I hadn't stopped using at this point in my life, I probably never would.

He described my future as a felon junky with no hopes and dreams. It was a bland future. It was depressing that he really thought I was going to keep using after this. In fact, so did I. This was terrifying. I wasn't supposed to be a felon. I finally realized I am a smart kid that a lot of people used to like. I have a good personality and a strong work ethic. Where did all these qualities go? I was baffled. I was beyond shocked that the most likely and safe outcome of my current situation was to go to prison for three years and keep doing dope.

My life for once came into perspective. I was fucked. I was so fucked and I didn't know what to do about it. I needed someone else to handle all this shit. I couldn't handle it. I needed someone else to tell me exactly what to do, step by step, and I would listen and do whatever they said. My friend from the program was not finished explaining my options. He said there was a small chance that I was ready to change my life and stop using heroin. He said if this could be a jumping off point and a way out, to take it. Don't think about how it will affect others if this is something that can help you straighten your life out. Then do the confidential informant thing and get the fuck out of town and into an inpatient rehab.

He explained how I must be really sick to think it a good idea to pick up a needle time and time again after the most traumatic things that happen when I do use. He was right. I was insane and my solutions were killing me. I needed to go to rehab. Was that even an option, I thought? Sure it was.

That conversation gave me hope. I was in a terrible place and I could use the pain and suffering as motivation to change my life. It was worth a shot after all. I had absolutely nothing left to lose. I called the police back and told them I would take the plea bargain if I could get to rehab as soon as it was over. He said he would talk to the district attorney and call me back. He called me back the next day and said that was fine. I would have to complete an in-patient rehab and do three undercover buys and the charges would be dropped. I was not allowed to use heroin or they would file charges. I had to go through withdrawals and buy heroin to turn over to the cops.

So unfair, I thought, but I was finally willing to do whatever it took to get out of town. The process dragged on and it was hard to catch the guy I was picking up from, because we had a system down that was very short and to the point. We talked numbers and specifics in person and never over the phone. This made it hard for the police. He never had it on him, which also made it hard.

I couldn't handle this. I wanted to get high so bad it was the only thing that would provide relief. I would stay up all night trying to devise a scheme to get just a little bit of dope from the buys to use. I tried to figure out how they would drug test me and if there was any way I could fake it. I spent hours trying to get high. Around this time, I called my parents and told my mother I was in trouble and I really wanted to go to treatment, but I needed help. She said there was a plane leaving shortly and asked if I wanted her to come out and help.

"Yes." More than anything I needed help. I was in over my head. I was trapped.

§

Please Come (Patty)

It had been fourteen years since my son's first drink. I looked down at my phone and read "please come" after asking if he would like some help moving out of his apartment in California and go to treatment in Utah. Within an hour of throwing my clothes into a small duffle bag, I hopped on a plane and traveled across the country to lend a hand. When I finally arrived in Mammoth Lakes, a desperate and disheartened 28-year-old greeted me. He had hit rock bottom. Fear, shame, and loneliness had overtaken him. He was in a dark hole, and for the following week, I dropped into it with him. I was there as a support. We worked hard to sort, sell, and discard his belongings. He had five sleeping bags, three sets of skis, and hoards of other paraphernalia.

While laboring to whittle down his belongings he was also smoking weed and drinking large amounts of alcohol. He was desperately dealing with heroin withdrawals and drinking all he could until he checked himself into treatment. As I sat in his apartment, witnessing my son's heartache, I couldn't believe this was my life. What happened to my little boy who loved building Legos and riding his bike? Where was my smart, tenderhearted little one who climbed trees and built tree houses? Why did he have so much pain and why couldn't I fix it?

Sitting in my own grief and pain, I knew I couldn't recommend the latest self-help book or therapist to make him well. I had a heavy heart but also great hope that he, in his pain, had chosen to get help. I was honored to be in the pain with him, coming alongside and helping him get to where he would find healing.

§

Legacy (Grayson)

I had a thousand thoughts flying through my brain at any given second and it was a challenge to let them go. My life was chaos. I was really good at things I never wanted to be good at. My medicine cabinet was full of prescription drugs from the doctor for withdrawals. I had over-the-counter medicine for withdrawals and countless herbal supplements and vitamins to help as well.

I was a pro at dealing with heroin withdrawals. It was just a part of my everyday life. So were misery, shame, and guilt. My tolerance for emotional pain was out of control. It was just my life. I heard someone tell me I deserved to get sober and I thought that was a strange thing to say. I deserved to die alone, I thought. Why did this person believe that I deserved the gift of sobriety?

After I completed my end of the plea bargain, I sold all my things and got on a plane to Utah to check into a wilderness therapy program. I was so excited to leave town. I was starting to have a little hope that this might in fact work. I had spent the last few weeks talking to a man who worked there about my situation. The love and support I received over the phone was overwhelming. I had someone on my side. For so long I didn't want anyone on my side. Now I was accepting anyone who could support me.

Before I got on the plane, I stopped at a liquor store and purchased nine mini bottles of Pendleton whiskey. To any real drug addict or alcoholic, this is the only logical way to fly even if I was going to a treatment center. It was a long day and I hadn't eaten anything. I met the man I had been talking to from the treatment center. His name was JP and he had a long beard like mine, but he had something I didn't. He had life in his eyes and a smile that made me want to be around him more. He greeted me with a burrito and a hug. He asked me if I had been drinking and I said I sure have. He seemed surprised that I was drinking, and I was surprised he had to ask.

When we got to the facilities, I felt like I could relax for the first time in years. No need to sleep with a loaded gun, because I was in the middle of southern Utah. I wouldn't have to worry about much of anything. For once in my life, I was excited to simply follow the rules and do as I was told.

I didn't sleep much the first night. I was nervous and excited. I knew I had a lot of work to do if I intended to stay sober. I knew I had to be honest about my life so these people could help me and that was scary. I was going to have to revisit some of the most painful times in my life if I was to get on the other side of them. I had never been more willing to do anything in my entire life. The willingness seemed to come out of nowhere and I was sure it would wear off. I was good at starting things and leaving them unfinished, and I was nervous this would be another one of those experiences.

As the days went on, my willingness gained momentum. My hope became more and more real that one day I could be free from the mental obsession every addict suffers from. I related to what I heard at the treatment center and saw how it applied to my life. I learned that the self-hate dialogue I had with myself was not the way everyone talks to himself. I was my own worst enemy. I hated myself and I learned how to change that. I hated the way I looked and the way I sounded. I told my therapist these things and he asked me why. We talked about it and I was honest about my childhood and now I don't hate the way I look or the way I sound. In fact I'm a tall handsome gentlemen who can't sing and that's fine.

I connected with other guys at treatment and it filled a part of me that was missing for so long. I wanted a role and I wanted connection. I was starting to get that in treatment and my momentum was building every day. Every day I worked on my problems, and to my amazement it did not tire me out. It gave me even more motivation to do the next right thing. All of a sudden, I was a person at the treatment center that could offer advice and comfort to the guy who just showed up. This was a new role for me as most of my life I didn't have anything genuine to offer in the way of help. It felt good and I wanted more of it.

The work I did with my therapist was the most beneficial part for me. With tears in my eyes, I finally told someone about being molested as a child. It was our first session and I didn't give a fuck. I was in a tremendous amount of pain and someone needed to hear this. I simply couldn't stand it anymore. His response was shocking. He looked me in my eyes and told me with deep sincerity that he was honored to be trusted with disclosure. He told me he was thrilled for me, because I was in a spot where I could be honest and walk through the pain. I had never thought about it the way he explained it to me. He encouraged me to share my story with other people in the group. I took his advice. Every single time I shared my experience, someone in the group would say - "me too." The more open I was about this, the more freedom I had. I could breathe again. Also, I wasn't getting high or drunk. I was just ok: it was a strange feeling at first. It was like waiting for a shock that never came or a plane crash that never did. I was waiting for something terrible to happen, but instead it was wonderful. It was counterintuitive. When I started to be honest with another man about my childhood experience, I began to heal. I had been guarding a wound for so long that I never let it heal. I tried to cover it up and it got infected until it almost killed me. The healing and growth that followed after being honest was quick and magical. I am not ashamed of my story anymore. It is just a part of who I am and I know there are so many people that have a similar experience who would benefit from being open and honest about it.

I told him about all of my insecurities and I followed through with all the assignments he gave me. He told me he loved me and I believed him. I loved him too. He was saving my life. My time at the treatment center was relatively short, 60 days, but they were full of tears and laughs and long adventures. It was the very beginning of my journey and I still had a lot of fears and anxiety when I got out.

§

Kleenex (Patty)

I'll never forget starting group therapy in 2010 with four other women and our therapist. I learned so much about being a co-addict and codependent. One time in particular when someone was in tears, a fellow member handed her a Kleenex. The therapist gently reprimanded the giver for two reasons. When someone is upset they need to learn how to do for themselves and reach out to get what they need, a Kleenex in this case. And secondly, when someone is crying and someone hands them a tissue it interrupts the moment, breaking the thought process and emotion. Respect others' struggles.

Same is true for other areas in which I need assistance. If I feel I need to talk to someone on the phone, then I need to make the call. Once in a meeting, someone said they needed people to call them. I disagree and think the person needing phone calls should make the calls himself. In essence, get their own Kleenex.

I've been told it's like a hula-hoop with me standing inside. The only thing I am responsible for is what is inside that hula-hoop. God will take care of what is on the outside.

I have learned to respect the struggle - respecting others' struggle and respecting my own struggle. I can recognize what I need and get my own Kleenex, and let you get yours.

§

Therapy Assignments (Grayson)

There have been a lot of incredible experiences in sobriety and I have had a hard time conveying their importance to me. I am naturally a very negative person, especially to myself. I have treated myself poorly. I often tell myself "I can't" or "I'm not good enough." My father is the same way and I think I learned a lot of these behaviors from him. I think he taught them to me unintentionally. I think I embraced them because the harder I was on myself the less of an effect my father had on me. If I was already a disappointment to myself then who cares who else is disappointed? This strategy helped me cope with a confusing and hurtful childhood. Although it wasn't all bad, I continually developed a way of living where I was always "less than."

When I arrived at Legacy Outdoor Adventures, this habit of mine was familiar and I had no idea it was atypical for someone to be that way. I had no confidences, and as a result, was addicted to drugs, living an unsatisfying life with no purpose. It was gloomy.

One of the most significant things I learned at treatment was how to be nice to myself. This made me laugh at first and my first thought was "Why should I be nice to myself? I am the one who fucked everything up." One negative thought is the beginning of many. My therapist gave me assignments that I thought were totally pointless and made me extremely uncomfortable.

The first week he told me that I needed to embrace the imperfections that I had. I told him some things about myself that I didn't like and I was convinced no one else did either. That week he encouraged me to wear my shirt inside out and backwards, leave my shoes untied, and only comb one side of my beard. This seemed crazy to me. I couldn't see the correlation. It was important to me to give off the appearance of someone who had his shit together even though I really did not. I had a long beard to hide my facial expression but I regularly combed it. This would be a challenge. I was willing to try anything.

I promised myself to do everything I was told at the treatment center. I told him how uncomfortable this was going to make me, and he said, "Great, that's the point. One last thing," he said, "don't tell anyone if they ask you why your shirt is inside out and backwards, you can't tell them it's your assignment." My anxiety went through the roof. I barely knew anyone else and my first impression was going to be disorganized and careless. Most of the field guides knew that I had once been a field guide myself. They would think I was full of shit because what field guide is going to go into the field looking like this?

I calmed my mind with other tools I learned in therapy. I went on a walk every morning by myself and began to tell myself that I could do it. I remembered to breathe throughout the day when I felt my anxiety increasing. I also journaled about the experience. It was hardly doable, but I did it. I completed my assignment. I was proud of myself and I wanted to tell everyone what I had just done. I wanted to know if my suspicions of everyone else judging me were right.

I was wrong. Everyone was wrapped up in their own shit. Only one person noticed my shirt being inside out and backwards and they thought I did it because I wanted to be different from the rest of the clients that were all wearing the same shirt. Not everyone was watching and judging me. This was life-changing. I had lived my life trying to figure out what other people were thinking about me. I was convinced others were judging me all the time. This was my first experience seeing that most people are too busy thinking about themselves to notice my small imperfections.

I was excited to get back to base camp and tell my therapist about my experience. Little did I know he was just getting started with his creative, useful, and indescribably uncomfortable therapy assignments. This was a guy who knew addiction. He was an addict. He knew how I thought. He knew I was a perfectionist and what this meant. He could tell from a few short conversations that I was living with a lot of shame and guilt. He knew this was related to being abused and possibly molested before I disclosed this to him. I trusted this man. After the first assignment, I knew he wasn't going to hurt me. I was going to do whatever he said would help me because he knew better than I did. I was excited to have someone so knowledgeable on my team. His name was Devon. He told me that he loved me after our third session - after only after three hours of conversation. He told me I could recover. He gave me hope. He also gave me a lot of uncomfortable therapy assignments.

The two assignments that helped the most had to do with me accepting affirmations from other people. I always thought if I got a compliment that the other party had a hidden agenda. They wanted something from me.

My first assignment was to give myself three affirmations at meal times in front of the whole group for a week. I couldn't think of this many affirmations for anyone. I was uncomfortable speaking in groups of people. I didn't like the attention. This was all my fears wrapped up in a therapy burrito. I hated it.

I hoped and wished the field guides would forget what I was supposed to do but they never did. Every meal before we ate, they would call on everyone to pay attention to my three affirmations. I did it. I came up with different ones every time; the assignment wasn't to believe them to be true. Simply just to state them. So I did.

As the week went on, I was more comfortable receiving affirmations from other people. Even when someone would thank me, I wouldn't believe them. This was slowly changing and I could see the difference. How incredible. I was excited for more therapy assignments. The more uncomfortable they were, the more growing I could do.

The next assignment was a doozy. Devon had me go around and ask each member for three affirmations at dinnertime. There were usually eight guys in a group, three affirmations each for seven days: 168 affirmations. I felt bad for everyone. I wanted to tell them they could lie just to make it easier for them, because there were nowhere that many affirmations to describe me.

Today, I don't think anyone lied. They didn't have much trouble coming up with nice things to say. At the time I thought some of these affirmations were not true and the giver simply didn't know me all that well. There was a second part of the assignment. For each affirmation I thought was false, I was to write about why it was true. Are you kidding me? If they told me I was athletic and I disagreed, I was to write about why I was, indeed, athletic.

This exercise surprised me and I changed my mind about a lot of things I thought about myself in that week. I was beginning to like myself. It became easier and easier to ask everyone for affirmations and the more time we spent together it was easier for them to give them. It was so counterintuitive, but I didn't spend so much time asking why it was working. I just wanted to know what I could do next and I would do it wholeheartedly. This was real. I was beginning to change. I was sober and I was working on the most important relationship I had and it was the one with myself. This was something I never thought of before. I started to consider my own feelings and needs. I had positive conversations with myself. I was very excited for who I was becoming.

§

Awfulizing (Patty)

Several years ago, my daughter came home for a few weeks. During her stay she went out with friends and ended up staying overnight with a girlfriend. I had tried texting with no response. Not knowing she had planned to be gone all night, I was in a sleepy state of awareness that she was not home. Drifting in and out of sleep, I commenced to plan her funeral. In my semi-state of consciousness I just know something dreadful had happened to her. I wasn't thinking straight. "No news is good news," I told myself. Finally, I learned my fears were in vain and she reappeared, thinking little of not telling me because she was used to being on her own. I had worsened the situation, making it the worst-case scenario.

I practice this from time to time, making matters worse in my head. Recently visiting my oldest son at rehab, I knew he had some childhood trauma to disclose. The few weeks leading up to our visit, I let my mind run wild with what had happened to him and how it would negatively impact his life forever. This was not the case; he had great resolution and freedom. I quickly learned that he worked through this horrific trauma and was now free and strong.

Why do I put myself through this mental and emotional torture? I believe if I imagine the worst-case scenario then it will lessen the blow. Through awfulizing, I try to control what may be and thereby make matters worse for myself.

Let go and let God, breathe and live in the moment. I'm finding freedom from compulsive worry.

§

Into Balance House (Grayson)

My time at treatment was fruitful. I was honest with everyone. I didn't get high, and every day I did the very best I could, all the way up to the last day. For a drug addict like me, finishing anything was a huge accomplishment. Sixty days of intensive inpatient care was a big deal. It was clear to me that this was just the very beginning, and I had a lot more work to do.

I didn't have any money. In fact I was about $9,000 in debt. My parents gave me $15,000 to get into treatment, which was less than half the cost. The treatment center gave me a scholarship. With no money and no plan, I was scared for my next step after treatment.

Before I went to treatment I had this idea that if I started this process, if I could just get my recovery rolling, it would gain momentum and doors would open. That is exactly what happened. It all started with talking on the phone with my now-good friend JP. He got me information for a scholarship for treatment. He picked me up from the airport. His phone calls saved my life. Now I was at another transition. I wanted to get into a sober living house. In fact, I thought I needed to.

I told my therapist exactly what I wanted to do when I got out. I wanted to get into sober living and start working construction in a couple weeks, hopefully, with people who understand and respect my recovery. I wanted to live in Salt Lake because there is a huge outdoor community there. I wanted to go to meetings. I wanted to get my vehicle out there in a couple weeks. I wanted access to my cell phone and the ability to live a responsible adult life in the structure of a sober living. I wanted to be drug tested and breathalyzed. I wanted to be held accountable for my actions.

One morning I was eating breakfast and my therapist came down to the dining hall to get me. I knew I was leaving soon, and my thoughts were distracted by females, tobacco, and coffee. When he told me he needed to talk to me, I was nervous that something with the courts in Mammoth got messed up and I was going to have to go to prison. My mind always went to the worst scenario.

It was totally opposite from that. He told me his good friend owned one of the most successful sober living houses in Salt Lake City. He said it cost about $3,000 a month. I couldn't come up with a fraction of that. My heart dropped but then he said the owner doesn't care how much you pay as long as you pay something and can be a positive influence around the house. I could hardly believe what I was hearing. I started to cry. I was going to be ok.

My needs were being met left and right as long as I was being honest about them. It was overwhelming to me that so many people did care. I felt undeserving and a little confused. This guy didn't know me, and he was willing to give up a bed at his sober living, which is usually full, so I could have a shot at a life worth living. This man who owns the sober living is in recovery and understands the hell that addicts live in. This man did a lot for me and our relationship would grow over the next few months, as he would take the time out of his day to take me out to lunch.

I was starting to see that there were so many people willing to help an addict in need. I was starting to learn how to allow other people to help me. I was beginning to get some confidence back. I was able to hold my head up a little higher. Things would continually get better from here.

§

Sponsor (Patty)

Once I found a twelve-step community, I was encouraged to get a sponsor and work the steps. I asked someone right away and she said she couldn't because she had not been through the steps herself. So, I asked another and another and for various reasons they were not available. I then got a phone sponsor from Michigan who said she would call me back in two hours and it's been six years.

Finally I settled on a lady in Al Anon, who was sweet and serene. She definitely had what I wanted, peace. She agreed to take me on and walked me through the steps. It was life changing. It caused me to take a deeper look at myself and why I did the things I did. It carried me to a deeper connection with God and living a life of purpose. There were times I would call her if I was in crisis and she would tell me to breathe. She taught me that every situation is an opportunity to trust God. With her guidance, I was able to let go of unhelpful thoughts and ways. She showed me what it's like to be a strong woman, owning my power and living from a principled place. It took me a while to find her, but I believe she was God-ordained.

Working the steps has better equipped me to handle life and live it fully. She helped equip me to sponsor others. And doing this service has further changed me. I have a front-row seat in watching God work in someone else's life. What an honor to be a part of such powerful, life altering work. I plan to take an active part in recovery for life. I will never graduate from working the 12 steps.

§

Balance House (Grayson)

I was proud of myself for doing most of the legwork to find a treatment center and completing it. I was proud to look back and say I did my very best while I was at treatment and there was nothing else left to be done. This was a new feeling for me and it gave me some confidence but I was also nervous. I was going to be living in a sober living house with 20 other people. There was not going to be very much structure at the sober living, which I was also excited about. I was nervous and excited to continue learning how to live a sober life. Having been in the rooms of Alcoholics Anonymous briefly, I knew AA would be a huge part of my recovery.

When I got to Balance House I met a man named Tony. I felt like he understood how uncomfortable I was within five minutes of talking to me. I met another tenant named Mike who had a Confederate flag tattoo on his left calf. This made me feel uneasy and I was quick to judge him. I was probably right.

My parents had come to Balance House to help me with my transition. Now it was time to say goodbye to my parents and unpack my things. What next? I thought. I had no plans. No one to call and almost everyone who lived at Balance House was at work. I was so uncomfortable in my own skin. I went on a walk. Going on a walk is always a good thing to do when I don't know what to do. My mother walks a lot in her free time and I thought of her when I decided to walk around town. I just needed to calm down and get some exercise. I let the man who was working at Balance know I was going to walk around. I walked for a little over an hour.

I went back to Balance House. Now what? I thought. This was proving to be harder than I imagined. I was lonely and bored. I needed friends and people to hang out with. I wanted a dog and a job. I wanted a vehicle. I was in debt over $9,000 and that occupied my mind. I tried to stay in the present and be grateful but it was a challenge. I missed my ex-girlfriend. I wanted to go to a meeting of Alcoholics Anonymous but I had no vehicle or friend to take me. I decided to watch some TV and wait for my other roommates to come home.

A couple hours later, the place filled up and was full of laughter. It was easy for me to make friends with the guys in my house and to tag along to a meeting. Then I met some ladies. This was a shocking experience to be around a member of the opposite sex, sober, and after not conversing with a lady for about two months. I felt my heart beat a little faster and I would often question what I was saying as I was saying it. Why was it so hard for me to have normal conversations with people?

There were a lot of people in that meeting and a lot of them introduced themselves to me. I got some phone numbers and started to feel less lonely and alone. I stood up to take my 60-day chip but I felt like it wasn't that big of a deal because I had been in treatment for all of it.

I was nervous to stand up in front of everyone and announce my name and how long I had been sober. The pretty girl named Ashley, whom I just met, would surely pay attention. Any chance of going on a date with her was out the window once she found out I was only 60 days sober.

I breathed through it and got my chip. The meeting was over. We stopped at a 7-11 on the way back to Balance House and I felt proud once again. Proud to be able to reach out and ask someone to take me to a meeting. Proud of myself for having a conversation with Ashley no matter how awkward it felt. I was being myself and I didn't need to feel bad about it or talk negatively about myself. I had nothing to be ashamed of.

I had to have these conversations in my head. I had to logically explain to myself that I was ok. I had to encourage myself and tell myself how proud I was of myself. This helped me to change into a more confident person. Anytime I would start to talk negatively about myself, I would stop and evaluate why. Usually I can steer the conversation in a positive direction and learn something. I do this a lot at work. I sometimes feel like I am less than most of the people at work. I am an equal person with fewer skills around concrete, because I have never done it before. There are some things that other people are better at and there are some things that I am better at. I have a lot of experience leading groups in the wilderness. I am good at it and have practiced it a lot. I am a hard worker, which applies to concrete even though I haven't learned the skills.

I also do this in my head when someone compliments me. The other day someone said that they appreciated my "go get 'em" attitude. I took offense because I thought he was being sarcastic. Most of my life I have not been a very enthusiastic person. I am calm and a lot of people guess correctly when they meet me that I like to smoke pot. I have that sort of temperament. So when he told me I had a real "go get 'em" attitude and he appreciated it, I thought he was being sarcastic and really meant something like I was being lazy. I stopped to think why he would say such a thing. I realized what I was doing. I was taking initiative at work and asking a lot of questions about how I can be helpful. He was not being sarcastic. I really am motivated to do my best and he could see that. I was pleasantly surprised. I was changing and people were starting to comment on it.

When I was at Balance House, they encouraged me to set goals for myself. They encouraged me to be a man of my word. If I can't keep my word to myself, then I can't do shit and I will surely relapse and live an unfulfilling life. I was taught that each time I didn't keep my word, a piece of my soul dies and eventually leads to a relapse.

I set easy goals for myself. I wanted to start flossing daily. I wanted to read daily. Making my bed was a goal. I also set a big goal of paying my credit card debt of $9,000 off in eleven months. I was firm in working toward these goals and started to become a man of my word. I slowly started to gain more confidence in the rooms of Alcoholics Anonymous. I have never called in sick or been late to work. I have been a loyal worker. I started to meet people in rooms of Alcoholics Anonymous. I kept doing the next right thing and asking for help and sooner, rather than later, I had friends.

I was climbing a lot and had friends who would call me to see if I wanted to do anything. This was certainly a drastic change from my lonely cold apartment building being sick from dope with little to no friends. I could hardly believe it was real. It was really happening for me. Everyone in AA told me the promises would come true if I worked the steps, but holy shit, this is more incredible than I thought. I suddenly felt like I was firing on all cylinders. Like my life was manageable again. Not only manageable but deeply satisfying.

§

Learning To Breathe (Patty)

I am learning to breathe, sitting with my pain, and breathing deeply. There are many helpful tools I have learned along this difficult journey that have helped me to survive and thrive even. One of the biggest lessons I have adopted is using "I" statements. This practice has been empowering. In my journey of recovery I have found my voice and one way I express it is using "I" statements. It is so helpful for me to speak up for myself and share my truth. Stating my reality and needs allows me to be strong and not be pushed around or manipulated by the people in my life. We teach people how to be in relationship with us and I have learned how to do this by being appropriately vocal. The addicts in my life have been master manipulators, so learning to take a stand has been revolutionary in my life.

Another word tool I have learned is to change "but" to "and." Anytime I use the word "but" 'or "however," I simply replace them with "and." This trick allows me not to minimize my story, pain or reality.

"I can't" has changed to "I am not willing." This keeps people from arguing or attempting to change my mind about whether I will help them or not.

"I have to" is now "I get to," putting a positive twist to activities in my life. Setting these phrases in motion enables me to take more ownership of myself.

Taking care of myself is now a priority. Allowing those around me to take care of themselves is also a priority. "Whose issue is it?" also helps me to let go of trying to take away an opportunity for people in my life to care for themselves.

Exercising self-care has recently become common practice in my life. Making sure I journal, walk, and call close friends are the main ways I care for myself.

Finding a sponsor and working the 12 steps has been a critical part of my own health and recovery. Attending 12 step meetings has been a lifeline to freedom, providing community and hope. Others in recovery truly understand my heartache and I learn healthy ways of coping with life's struggles.

§

What It Is Like Now (Grayson)

Going to a treatment center helped me more than I can describe. Living at Balance House set me up to live a successful, sober life that is fulfilling. I can't tell you exactly when it happened, but I finally had a spiritual experience. It was clearly a result of working the 12 steps. Every Sunday I would go over to my sponsor's house and read the *Big Book*. He would read it and I would listen. I knew when I heard this man share at a meeting that he had something I desperately wanted. Being sober was not enough. I didn't know how to live a sober life and this man would help me do that.

We read the book and did what it said. By taking action and trying to grow spiritually through prayer and meditation, the obsession to get high or drunk left me. I no longer obsess about a drink or a drug. After years and years of constantly thinking about these things, I found freedom. This is what everyone in the program was talking about. It is a miracle that an addict like me who lived a life too enthralled by everything to do with drugs isn't thinking about it anymore. Peace and serenity are a part of my life. They are things I had been searching for years. I never knew it could be this easy. It is simple. I didn't believe the promises would come true for me when I first heard about them in the meeting but I was willing to give it a shot. I had the gift of desperation and I was willing to try anything. I didn't believe in God and thought that would disqualify me from a spiritual experience but it didn't. My experience is that you don't have to believe in God to live spiritually.

Today I am honest with everyone in my life - my employer, my friends, and most importantly myself. When I wake up, I ask God to help me and at night I give him thanks. I don't know who God is or what God is but I was taught to do these things, so I do them.

I have fulfilling relationships. I am a part of something. For most of my life, I never fit in. There was always something wrong with me. I don't feel like that anymore. That is the spiritual experience. All my life, I felt like a worthless piece of trash and now I don't. I take suggestions from people whom I want to be like. I surround myself with people whom I look up to. For most of my life I cut myself off from successful people, because I wasn't successful. I was told that I am the sum of the five people I spend the most time with. I believe that to be true and the people I spend the most time with all have something I want and live life to the fullest.

I have received two raises in the past six months at work. I simply show up on time and work. No more having to leave early to get a bag of dope. No more calling in sick when I'm dope sick. My life is incredibly more satisfactory and easy going.

I have genuine friendships. People tell me they love me and I tell them I love them. I have never had that and always wanted that. I am good friends with the man who picked me up from the airport and drove me to the treatment center. He lives in Salt Lake City and we climb often. More than that, we share our hearts with each other. Climbing is secondary. Having someone to be vulnerable with about my struggles and who I am is a gift and I cherish it. I get phone calls now from friends who ask me to hang out, to go to a meeting, or just to say hi. I used to wonder why I even had a phone because no one ever called. These relationships mean the world to me. Most of my life I didn't want to be vulnerable because I thought everyone was out to get me. Today, I know this is not true. I have an amazing circle of friends who are fun and enjoy my company.

I have always wanted to be dependable. Most of my life I haven't been. My experience with recovery and the 12 steps taught me how to be dependable. People can call me when they are having a hard time and I show up for them. Me, the heroin junky, has a lot to offer when I am clean and sober.

I have had insomnia since I was 15. However, the first time I took sleeping pills it was to get high, and then I convinced myself I needed them to sleep. I took sleeping pills for over 10 years. I supplemented them with benzos, alcohol, and heroin to just get a few precious hours of sleep. When I went to treatment I took Trazodone, a non-narcotic prescription medication that helps with sleep. All my life I had to make sure I would have enough for trips or there was a pharmacy nearby so I could get a refill. Thanks to the gifts of peace and serenity, I no longer need to take prescription meds to go to sleep. This amazes me. In such a short time I was relieved from everything. I could sleep eight hours a night and awake feeling restored. I had been trying to do that for years. I was certain that at the very least I would smoke pot for the rest of my life to get some good sleep. I no longer need it and the freedom is overwhelming.

My life is in order after a short time working the 12 steps of Alcoholics Anonymous. My life is fulfilling and exciting. I get to do all the things I love like skiing in the backcountry, rock climbing, and mountain biking. Working the 12 steps has provided me with the peace and serenity I sought through drugs and alcohol. Today, I am completely clean and sober. My mind is calm and I laugh a lot more. My hope is that other addicts who can relate to me will give the program a shot. On one side is a sick and twisted disease; on the other side is abundant freedom.

§

Choices (Patty)

I have choices. And recognizing this helps me to be more intentional with my time and relationships. I can choose what I want on my plate. I have the ability to make choices in all areas of my functioning: physical, emotional, and spiritual, and I want my choices to be God directed.

I have gotten better at saying "no." It has not been easy but I have pushed through. I have learned to say, "No, but thanks for asking." I ask myself if it is something I *can* do or give and if I am *willing* to do or give it *freely*?

Years ago I played on a tennis team that was loads of fun. We laughed and played hard and always went to lunch after. Then I was bumped to a higher team and began playing with women much more serious and even crude at times. I hung in there, missing my former team. Then, things began to unravel in my family and life's pressures increased. I realized I was not enjoying tennis anymore. Why was I continuing to play when it no longer served to be pleasurable? It dawned on me that I had a choice to quit and I did. What a relief. I do have choices and am in charge of what activities to participate in.

Spiritually, I can choose how to pursue my relationship with God and what works for me. I have greatly simplified and cut back on my involvement in obligatory church activities and now seek more individual pursuits of God. Cutting back in this area has given me a stronger connection with God. And my faith community is smaller and more intimate.

Emotionally, I have set healthy boundaries with people I choose to be in relationship with. I recognize safe people and want to surround myself with healthy people. I realize I become like those I choose to hang around, so it's important to choose wisely.

Physically, I have learned to take charge of my health. I choose healthier foods and physical activity, and also make time for Epsom salt baths.

My choices about my physical, emotional, and spiritual life affect others. All these areas are integrated. I know I have choices and that I'm worth it.

§

Detach With Love (Patty)

I used to get multiple phone calls from my youngest son during the height of his addiction. He called when he needed something, usually needing money (for food, of course), a ride, or to do his laundry at my house. I would try helping and giving (I love giving) and my loving generosity compounded the situation. I remember hearing AA speakers share their stories and more than not, the story included "when my mom stopped ..." So, I stopped. I stopped rescuing my son from his troubles. Learning about detachment, I began detaching.

One time stands out when he was desperate and hungry. I'm his mom and felt burdened and caught between a rock and a hard place. So, I made soup and took some to him. Sweet potato chili was a way I could detach with love. He really needed money and I was not willing to give him money, and I was not willing to let him go hungry.

I learned to stop engaging him. When he called I would say, "I know you know what to do, I know you'll figure it out." One time he called needing to talk to someone, and I said, "Yes you need to talk to someone, but it's not me." He stopped calling. I felt empowered when I realized I teach people how to be in relationship with me. I realized how, in my behavior through detaching, he was given the space to take responsibility for his own life. Wow, I can control what I am willing to do for someone else, and setting appropriate boundaries is important. He could not figure it out if I kept figuring it out for him.

I am full of good ideas and love passing them along. I would generously share these ideas with my kids in order to "help"- helping them find their way through life. They don't need my help, and my advice only helped keep them stuck. They have a brain and a higher power; they are quite capable to take responsibility for their own lives. By giving them answers, I was robbing them of the dignity and self-esteem to figure it out themselves. I stopped needing them to need me.

Detachment meant declining to engage in the drama of the life of an addict. An invitation onto the crazy train was common until I learned I had a choice and could decline boarding.

I am free - free from taking on others' "stuff." I can live my life and let them live theirs.

§

Sobriety Gave Me What Drugs And Alcohol Couldn't (Grayson)

In sobriety, I have found everything I was looking for with drugs and alcohol. Sobriety has been very counterintuitive, which is why it is important that I have other people in my life tell me exactly how they did it. Today, I am amazed at all the good things in my life. All my life I wanted to fit in so badly and I thought by smoking pot it would give me some common ground with other people. I thought it gave me purpose, to grow pot and sell it. People depended on me and would call me daily.

It only took a short while before I felt like I was being used. No one wants to hang out with their drug dealer anyway. I thought psychedelics would offer me insight into what meaningful relationships were supposed to look like. I had some good times but all in all it was confusing and it didn't help me establish any meaningful relationships. Through Alcoholics Anonymous and working the twelve steps I have meaningful relationships today. I have people I can call when things are tough, and I have people I can call when things are going great. For the most part, things have exceeded my expectations and I have been filled with joy and disbelief. It is wonderful to have people to call and explain how things are going and for them to be able to relate to my experience.

I am honest today, which is key to meaningful relationships. I no longer use people for connections or money. I hang out with people I look up to. I hang out with people who encourage me to be a better person and hold me accountable for my actions.

I always struggled with what my purpose was. Today, my purpose in life is to enjoy it and to show other alcoholics and addicts that there is freedom from addiction. I do this by taking care of myself and doing the things I enjoy. I have more time to climb, bike, ski, and do all the outdoor activities that give me pleasure. I have passion today and it is exciting. I thought drugs and alcohol could fill that void, but they only separated me from any purpose and meaning. This created a vicious cycle that deepened my feeling that life was without meaning.

Looking back on my romantic relationships is one of the more counterintuitive areas to examine. I thought if I had some pills and weed to take the edge off, then my partner would be more attracted to me. I thought it made me more entertaining. They did take the edge off and I thought this helped me communicate when actually it always led to lies and deceit. I was trying to be someone I was not.

Today I don't have to fight that battle. I can embrace who I am without drugs and alcohol and I like who I am. I can show up in my own skin and I don't feel the need to convince people I am a certain way. I have nothing to hide today and the freedom is indescribable.

I tried to make a lot of money by selling drugs. I sold plenty but seemed to never have enough cash. Today, I don't sell any drugs and I have plenty of money to do the things I love. I have plenty to pay rent and all my utilities. I bought a puppy and I can afford to take her to the vet and buy her food and all the best chew toys Petco has to offer. My biggest financial accomplishment is paying off $9,000 of credit card debt.

Money consumed my thoughts when I was drinking and using. In the later years of addiction, I would try to buy pills with money orders that I used my credit card for and make a profit selling them to pay off the debt. I failed time after time and the debt grew and grew. I could never get a grip on it. In my short period of sobriety I have been diligent about making payments. Slowly I have paid it all off and the freedom is refreshing. It should be known that I don't make six figures. I get paid hourly as a general laborer for a concrete company. I had help from the owner of Balance House to set up a budget to be able to pay it off. I stuck to the plan.

All areas of my life have improved greatly. I live an exciting life. It is exciting because I am beginning to see my full potential. I feel like I can do whatever I want if I stay sober. I have people in my life who are more than willing to help get the things I want out of life. I love to build things. From Lincoln logs to Legos to snow shelters to the fence in my parents' backyard, I love to build things with a purpose. I get a lot of satisfaction from it. I have a mind that understands math. I want to be an engineer. I never felt like I was smart enough or good enough to pursue such a challenging degree. I will start school in a couple weeks working towards a degree in Civil Engineering from the university of Utah.

Today, I believe I am smart enough and driven enough to complete the program. Even just going through the application process and being accepted was a huge accomplishment. When I was drinking and using, the smallest tasks would leave me baffled and I could never finish. Today, I am able to see things to the end. The more I practice this, the better I am at finishing the task at hand.

Every single thing I wanted drugs and alcohol to do, sobriety has done for me. I am amazed at how this has worked. It doesn't make a lot of sense to me, but that doesn't matter. What matters is that it is true for me, and I couldn't be more thrilled to live the life I have today. It took a lot of work and that is why it has been so satisfying.

I Let Go (Patty)

I'm a nice and thoughtful person. Having a knack for picking up on other people's discomfort comes second nature to me. I'd swoop in and take care of those around me. I spent years in my marriage caregiving, believing it's what a wife's role should be. Relieving my husband's anxiety was my job as was taking care of my kid's problems. I worked very hard to help others in need.

What I came to see was how my generosity to those in need benefitted me. Relieve someone else's anxiety and I relieve my own. Simply put, if the people around me were uncomfortable, so was I. Showering others with gifts and kindness gave me purpose as well. I let go of a lot of that. Recovery taught me that over-functioning on behalf of others who could and should do for themselves is liberating. I am not responsible for relieving others' anxiety.

I have a mental piece of paper with two columns. In one column I list what I'm responsible for, things I can change or do, and in the other column is a to-do list for the universe. These mental images allow me to let go of worry and control, liberating me from things I have no control over.

§

Looking Back ... Little Bro (Grayson)

My brother and I were inseparable when we were young, playing tackle football and building forts out of anything. We were best friends. I also felt a sense of responsibility for his safety and how others treated him. He was my little bro. No one fucks with him except me.

My brother and I are very close. We also couldn't be more different. He is the life of the party. He seems to talk to ladies with ease. He is talkative. He knows what clothes to wear and what to order at a restaurant.

Most of our bonding and growing together has been over smoking pot together. It was what we did, before and after everything. It was exciting and fun. It helped on family vacations. It helped on plane rides and car rides. We were always "taking a walk" before Thanksgiving meals or before Christmas Eve dinner. In the beginning we were cautious and used eye drops, gum, and plenty of Axe body spray. In our adult years we stopped caring so much. It also stopped being fun and became more of a hassle, more of an obligation. There were many arguments over who threw down more bud or who was taking bigger hits. It never seemed fair or satisfying. We annoyed the shit out of each other. I used my brother to sell the pot I would drive back from Colorado. I would give him some for giving me people to sell to. It didn't matter how much I gave him. In a couple of days he wanted more. He thought I never gave him a fair amount. I thought he was selfish and never satisfied.

I always wanted my younger brother to think I was cool. I used drugs and alcohol to gain his respect. The first time I tried cocaine I got it from my next-door neighbor. She gave me a little bag and said to do as much as I wanted and I could pay her the next day when she could see how much I had used. It was off-white and shiny. The little flakes stuck together. It was different from what I thought it should be. It had a strong smell. I thought it was white powder and no smell.

I did a little bit and my heart took off. I began panting and I couldn't wait to tell my little bro what I had. I went to his room where he was in bed. I think I was in the ninth grade and he was in the eighth. I told him I had some cocaine that I got from our next-door neighbor. We stayed up all night and did all the cocaine in the bag. It was magnificent.

My drug use took off from there and so did his. We no longer hung out like best friends do. We distanced from each other. I went to a different high school and started playing football. My brother was reckless and started partying more. I was a responsible drug user. He was not.

I went off to college and our relationship became increasingly distant. I heard that he was getting more into pills and heroin. I was, too, but I was sure I was more responsible about it. His drug use started to frighten the whole family and this took the attention off me. I came home to visit for a month after graduating college and I went to his house. I knew he was doing dope. I was clean for a brief period of time but I wanted to use more than anything. This would be a wonderful excuse. I went to his house and his girlfriend was home. We smoked a bowl on the couch and played some music. He showed me what he was into and I shared some of my favorite music.

His girlfriend left to go to work and as soon as that door closed my brother bolted from the couch to the bathroom. I knew what that meant. I had been there many times before. My brother was trying to hide it from me because he knew I was clean at the moment. I told him I knew what he was doing and asked if I could buy a little bit. He expressed his concern but said if I wanted to that he could get it. I just wanted to do one shot. Plus, it was white heroin. I had never done white heroin. It seemed like a perfectly good reason to relapse. I did a shot in his house and the mental obsession took over. I needed more. I didn't give a fuck about connecting with my brother I just used him to get more dope and pills. That led to a month long binge of shooting cocaine and dope which landed me in the hospital.

It was a sad situation. My brother and I used to have fun together. We could entertain ourselves for hours and make each other laugh hard. We were fun to be around. We had something to offer. That was all over and it made my heart hurt. I felt like a horrible example. I had failed from keeping my brother safe. The reality set in. We were junkies going nowhere.

§

Brothers, How Things Are Now (Grayson)

I want to tell you how things are now because it is unbelievable. After I decided to get sober I started talking to my brother more. I was sad because he was still using. I knew I couldn't hang out with him if he was using and I was trying to stay clean. I wanted things to be like they were when we were younger. That just wasn't going to happen if one of us was using.

I was in sober living and he was still doing dope. We had some conversations about sobriety and using. I asked him why he wasn't going to get sober and he told me he thought he would be missing out. I understood this thought process. We continued to talk. I knew he was about to break up with his girlfriend of a few years. I was hopeful this would be a jumping off point for him to get some help.

He started trying to sell heroin. He was open and honest with me and I could tell he was in a spot I had been in not too long ago. Not long after that, he decided to go to treatment. I was so excited. I knew that in sobriety our relationship could be restored and we could have fun together again. We could joke. My brother is one of the most fun human beings I know, not when he is trying to put needles in his arm though. I am happy that he is sober today. We talk on the phone every few days about sobriety and girls.

A few months ago we were together at my parents' mountain house near Asheville. There was a concert he wanted to go see. I didn't know who the band was, but I knew if my brother liked it, it would be good. If he was sober and I was too, it would be fun. We danced and talked to girls in costumes and had a good time. We laughed and made fun of each other. We were in the moment and loving it. It was a big deal to me, to be able to hang out with my little bro completely clean and sober. He is a blast to be with. I love you brother.

§

My Family (Grayson)

Let me tell you about my family. My father attends 12-step recovery. My mother is a chocolate addict (yes that is a real thing) and my brother and I are drug addicts. My sister is an addiction counselor. It runs deep in my family. We each have our own special addiction and it has set up barriers. It has blocked us off from connecting with one another. I have heard people say that the opposite of addiction is not sobriety: it is human connection. I think this is true. Each member of my family has failed to form bonds with other humans, so we turned to substances, food, or intimacy in other forms. I can speak for all of us and say that we wanted human connection. We found something that was more appealing at first sight.

Today, we are all in recovery. We have all found something to restore the ability to be vulnerable and connect with one another. It has been a rewarding experience for me. I can talk to every member of my family about private issues and get helpful feedback and support. I have a relationship with them all that is envied by most. I am grateful to have grown up in a family like this. I would have never learned about this way of living unless I was a drug addict. I would never have been willing to go through the steps of Alcoholics Anonymous.

My dad used to make me go to church when I was a little kid. I hated it.

It is one of the worst memories of my childhood. It was boring and uncomfortable. I hated shaking hands with his friends. I would watch the clock slowly tick by and the worst Sundays were when the pastor went past 12. It was almost unbearable. I didn't like to have friends over Saturday night because if they stayed with us they would have to go to church with us.

When I was 20 I moved to Colorado to get away from the "Bible Belt." I was sick of it. When I was 22 Dad called and asked if I had a minute to talk. This was already strange, as we didn't talk very much. He went on to apologize for making me go to church. I thought it was a trap. I hadn't heard this man admit his wrongs. He told me the way he behaved was wrong. This was shocking to hear and I didn't know why he was telling me. It meant a lot to hear him admit his wrongs. I didn't view him as weak for doing so. It was quite the opposite. I had respect. It was a heartfelt apology and I felt respected. It was wonderful. I felt like he was opening up to me a little bit, something that has always been a struggle for him. He was making amends.

I did not know this at the time but he was in his 12-step program doing what his sponsor had suggested and I think his decision to do so set in motion recovery for the whole family. I will never forget that phone call as long as I live. He opened up to me and was vulnerable. Now I felt a little more comfortable doing the same thing. Over the next few years, this sort of behavior became more apparent and natural. We started hugging more in person and it wasn't uncomfortable. Slowly this man, my father, who I didn't want to be anything like, became my biggest role model.

Today, I cherish his advice. I want what he has. If you don't think people change, then you haven't met anyone like my father. His anger is gone. He is happy. He is calm. He has fun and laughs. It is a miracle. It is a result of the 12 steps. The 12 steps come in many different shapes and sizes, but I'm sure it works no matter how you get there. The promises came true for my dad and witnessing that was a huge part in my decision to seek out recovery. I have a great time with him today and talk to him whenever I have a free moment.

My mother is addicted to chocolate. When she first told me this I was offended. How could you say you are an addict and you haven't been through the hell of withdrawals or mental obsession I have? How can she claim to have the disease of addiction with a piece of candy? Drugs and alcohol led me to compromise my life. I was sure chocolate could not lead anyone to the bottom I experienced. Maybe that is true but it is not important. The important part is spiritual. She formed a bond with chocolate that cut her off from growing spiritually. I did the same thing with drugs and alcohol. We had the same spiritual malady and the same solution - working the 12 steps. When I saw the promises come true for her is when I fully accepted that it does not matter what a person is addicted to. It matters that they are maladjusted to life and cannot form relationships with others.

Today she hasn't had chocolate for years and her life has changed. She laughs more. She has more friends. She has hobbies and goals. She is a joy to be around. Her happiness no longer depends on the happiness of others. She is comfortable with who she is. Recovery has given us a common language and a way to relate. It has provided us with a common language. It has given us hope.

I already wrote about my brother; the same is true for us. We can have a relationship now because of recovery. My sister is not an addict. I don't know how she survived childhood. I joke with others and say that she is smart and strong because she had to grow up with addicts for brothers. I think this is true. She is by far more intelligent and mature than my brother and I. She is the youngest and is a successful counselor in the field of addiction. It cracks me up that everyone in my family is an addict except my sister, who is a therapist.

We talk a lot about addiction and its language. We share experiences and hope. I value her opinion above most others. She's intelligent and it's apparent in the way she talks about addiction. I look up to her even though she is younger. She is wise and has been intentional about setting boundaries with the addicts in her family. Her healthy lifestyle has affected the rest of the family. I learned that families are similar to a wheel on a bike. If there is a spoke that is loose it will throw the other spokes out of whack. When one spoke gets tightened or tuned correctly it will force the others to either break or be tightened. Through recovery, every member of my family has been a spoke on the wheel that has been adjusted to work. Today, we are a somewhat functional wheel.

Every Sunday at 7:30 p.m. (EST), we all get on the phone. We do a family check-in. It's our way of staying connected and up-to-date on how everyone is doing. We usually share how we are feeling, what our past week was like, and what goals we have for the following week. I am so grateful I have a family with whom I can do this. We all have individual passions and goals, and it is such a blessing to be a part of my family members' lives. I cherish these phone calls and I am grateful for a family that has chosen recovery. It has been a wild ride, but I wouldn't change anything. I am glad we are where we are today.

§

Play Then, Play Today (Patty)

I distinctly remember when I got a yellow, ten-speed Schwinn bike. Riding my bike was invigorating. The many hills in our suburban neighborhood provided the thrill of a rollercoaster. I felt free, wind blowing in my hair and the sun on my face. I rode for fun. Playing outside was constant and if I was not biking, I was running over to a friend's house.

I played outside all the time, calling my best friend to come out and play. We went down to the creek for hours, making an island in the water with little make-believe settlers.

I played tackle football with the boys on the lawn in front of the school, inhaling the fragrance of grass when lying face down on the ground after a tackle ... getting the dried, brown grass all over my clothes and in my hair.

Swimming and tennis filled my summers and hours were lost doing these activities.

So, how do I play today? What activities do I do where I lose track of time? I still get a burst of energy and choose to run to get where I'm going. I much rather play a sport than watch it. I love interactive games like charades or Pictionary. There is nothing like getting lost in a good book. I like being around people who make me laugh. I make a conscious effort to keep laughter and play in my life. Doing something I love to do everyday proves life-giving. If you want to visit with me, I'll ask if we can walk. There's nothing better than walking while we visit together.

§

Al Anon, Help & Perspective (Patty)

I exhibited symptoms of PTSD due to living years with addicts, and looking for signs of using or signs of sobriety. I am acutely aware of facial expressions and voice inflections. I've been observing my children their whole lives - watching for bloodshot eyes, listening for the pain in their voices, and smelling alcohol on their breath.

Recently visiting my son, I noticed that I smelled him. Who does that? Apparently, I've done this his whole life and just came to realize my behavior. He had the faint smell of coffee on his breath where I used to detect alcohol. His clothes smelled clean and no longer reeked of pot. This habit of mine comes with the territory of being a mother, watching for eye contact and overall demeanor. Is he happy and living up to his potential?

It was so nice to finally find Al Anon where I learned about the "Three C's". I did not Cause it, can't Control it, and can't Cure it. I apply the

"Three C's" to the addict's behavior and to everybody else's I'm in relationship with. The slogans "Let go and Let God" and "Live and Let Live" also help me apply the "Three C's". These principles help me let go of trying to control others.

Al Anon has greatly aided my continued recovery, helping me to deal with my triggers. Through Al Anon I learned how to handle my PTSD and trust God with caring for my triggers. Al Anon gives me the help and perspective I need when I smell my children. I can let go.

§

Sense Of Self (Patty)

When I was a little girl, I wanted to be just like my best friend, Lauri. I envied her long, straight, blond hair and her petite, slender body. I had dark brown hair that always seemed to have tangles and an athletic body that would never be lanky. She had two beautiful older sisters while I had brothers. Everything she had and did was cool. She had a million pets with the coolest names. She was so creative and clever.

We had a lot of fun and laughed a lot. One time we decided to get a bowl of her dad's homemade matzo ball soup. While retrieving the large pot from the fridge we dropped it and soup went all over her kitchen floor. We worked hard with lots of paper towels sopping up all the liquid. We placed the matzo balls back in the pot and returned it to the fridge in hopes no one would notice. Her dad, of course, noticed that his prized soup had no broth. He was furious. Thinking we could get away with that still brings us laughter.

I wanted to be her and not me. Anything that was her favorite became my favorite. I even got a blond doll for Christmas just like hers, not thinking I could have gotten the brunette version.

As an adult I continued to make choices like those around me. My home decor was a mixture of various items people had given me, a mishmash of silver, brass, and wood. Formal and casual push-abouts filled my shelves. It was not until a decorator friend came over and gave me "permission" to take away the things that were not "me." What do I like? I began setting out the things I like and decorating the way I wanted, not what was expected of me. I no longer had to be what others thought I should be or what I assumed others wanted me to be. I had a growing sense of self, flourishing in my individualism.

Recovery has provided even more self-actualization and growth. I am more aware of who I am and what I like. Recently, when building a mountain home I was able to express my taste. I chose the brunette doll.

§

Hope For The Future (Grayson)

Happy, joyous and free. Peace and serenity. Being able to handle situations that used to baffle me. The *Big Book of Alcoholics Anonymous* talks about these things. When I first read it, they meant nothing to me. They were silly little sayings that people in the program used to convince me that I needed recovery. Today, these words have a lot of value in my life. Today, I understand what they mean and how precious they are. I was willing to do anything to stay sober when I went to treatment and began my journey of recovery. I didn't think I would end up living a much more fulfilling life. I did it because I didn't want to go to jail. I didn't want to die. I didn't know how to deal with the heartache of a break-up. I did not get sober because I thought it would be a blast. I didn't get sober because I thought I would be calmer.

Almost everything I first thought about sobriety was wrong. It is much more simple compared to the way I was living when I was drinking and using. There is a lot less confusion and the voices in my head have nearly gone silent. I am learning to do the next right thing as I go through each day. I listen to my conscience and to people I respect. I am honest because I have to be. It is one of the principles of the twelve steps and it helps keep me sober. That's it. I am not honest because I was born that way; I'm honest for selfish reasons. It helps me sleep at night.

In sobriety, I have set goals for myself. I do this because now I feel like I am living a life that is going somewhere. It is not just a meaningless dead-end road. I have passions and I want to do great things and be successful. One of my first goals I set was to floss everyday. You might think this is a trite goal. However, for a drug addict like me, it is quite the accomplishment to do anything at all on a consistent basis. This is where I started. This was my first goal. Today, I don't even think about it. I just floss. I get a little more confidence every time I follow through with one of my goals.

When I first arrived at my sober living house, I talked with one of the owners about my future. "Now that I am sober what on earth am I going to do with myself?" My days were spent at bars and trying to cop dope. My life revolved around the dealer's schedule. I had no life. Now I will have a lot more free time and energy to spend somewhere else. I wanted to go back to school but I was nervous to share that with him. It seemed out of the realm of possibilities for me. For some reason, I felt like I was not good enough to go to school.

I told him anyway. He helped me get information about which school to apply for and helped me apply. Today I am studying Civil Engineering. I have found that school is even much easier when I am sober. I don't forget things like I did in school when I was drunk and high all the time. I can study for longer periods, even without Adderall - and there is no crash.

I am still working at the same place I worked when I first got out of treatment. It isn't as hard as I thought to juggle school and work. I don't need to make sure I have enough pills for the day. It is not a part of my morning any more. Instead, I simply ask God for help or the universe or whatever might be persuaded by my willingness. I show up to work, usually about 15 minutes early. I have done this every day. I have received countless compliments on my work ethic. People tell me that everyone really enjoys working with me. I tell you this because it never happened when I was using, only when I got sober.

Since I started working I have been able to always do my best. The superintendent has noticed it, and I have received two raises. It is because of this that I was able to pay off $9,000 of credit card debt. The freedom from being debt free is motivating. Sobriety has really paid off.

The best part about sobriety is my mental health and personal relationships. What has happened with my relationships? I am able to connect with other humans. This was something I always wanted, but had such a hard time getting. When I was drunk or high, I could not connect with others even though that was my goal. I was confused and believed drugs and alcohol helped me connect. It took me years to see that it had the opposite effect. Now I have meaningful friendships. I have friendships where we support each other and talk about life. I have never felt like someone had my back like I do now. I have the confidence to ask girls out. I haven't fallen in love yet and that is probably for good reason. However, the excitement of asking a girl out on a date and having a good time with a member of the opposite sex is thrilling and it restores my confidence. I am a good person that people want to spend time with when I am sober. This change is a lot more clear to me and others.

The biggest gift of all and the things that make all the above possible are peace and serenity—the change between my ears. To understand this, you must know what it is like to be obsessed about something. To know the type of obsession that doesn't go away unless you give into it. The type that is all consuming and all powerful. For me it was drugs and alcohol. If I wasn't using, I was obsessing about it. The only way to make it stop was to give in.

Alcoholics Anonymous has shown me another way to live that has replaced the obsessive thinking. I don't know when it happened exactly, but I know it was a result of working the 12 steps with a sponsor I had a lot in

common with. At some point while working with him, I would go all day
without thinking about smoking cocaine or shooting dope. I even stopped
having "using" dreams. That was shocking. With all this extra brain energy,
I could do something really helpful and constructive - like write a book! My
life has changed drastically. I am a completely different person. I have some
of the same passions like skiing and rock climbing, but the way I deal with
people is completely different. None of it was my idea. It was all
suggestions I got from people in AA or the *Big Book* itself.

Today, I continue to set goals for myself and with each goal I reach, I
gain a little more confidence and realize I can actually do whatever I want. I
can make a plan and do anything.

To stay sober the rest of my life there are a few simple things I'm
convinced I must do. I need to go to meetings. I have heard it said a
thousand times when someone comes back from a relapse that they
stopped going to meetings. I hope I can learn from their mistakes and make
meetings a consistent part of my life. I think they are a lot of fun anyway,
and I enjoy some of the people I have met there. I must work with other
alcoholics and pass this thing along. This will help me stay sober, because I
believe my purpose and the biggest reason I got sober is to help someone
else. It is a domino effect and I hope that I stay sober and continue to
influence things in a positive directions.

I intend to graduate from the University of Utah with a bachelors degree
in Civil Engineering and build things. I want to be in charge of big projects
in Salt Lake City and oversee their development. I have a yellow lab, Lady,
and I intend to spend a lot of time with her exercising outside and teaching
her how to follow me on backcountry ski tours. I will continue to try new
things.

The *Big Book* talks about one thing that cuts us off from a spiritual
experience and it is contempt prior to investigation. There are many things
I have not tried that until I try them I don't know if I like them or not such
as yoga. I was convinced beyond a shadow of a doubt that I hated yoga. It
was too hard to follow the instructions. I didn't like being in a room with
that many people. I am not flexible. I can't do the poses. Well, I tried it in
sobriety, and I absolutely love it. I gave it an honest shot and the payoff was
great. Some of the things I said about yoga in the past make me laugh. They
are ridiculous and I had no idea what I was talking about. I try to remember
this when someone asks me to try something I have never tried before. In
order to stay sober I need to keep an open mind and be willing. I need to
say "yes" more.

For me, the work I have done in sobriety has paid off more than I can
describe. It is fascinating that people with considerably more time than I
have keep telling me to keep coming back (to meetings). That it will get
even better. Impending doom has been replaced with hope and excitement.

The terror I experienced on a daily basis has been replaced with joy and freedom. These changes are real in my life today and the result of working the 12 steps with a sponsor.

My body and mind have recovered. I thought for sure I would have some lasting complications. I know I can work longer and harder when I am sober. It is very clear to me now. My memory has gotten a lot better, which plays a huge part in being productive at work and in building meaningful relationships.

§

Living In Freedom (Patty)

Our family gatherings used to always be stressful. Pot was always present then and I often reiterated my boundaries around pot in my house when the boys came to visit. I accepted the fact that I was not going to change their minds around the "health benefits" of pot. And the drinking! I would just turn in early to avoid being around anyone who had had too much to drink. I operated out of self-protection and fear. I experienced sadness at the lack of connection with the addicts in my life.

Then I chose recovery, all of us chose recovery, and our gatherings have changed. Connection has replaced being checked out, and we now take part in fun group activities. I've seen my sons initiate some of the activities and conversations. I like being around them now. I love hearing the family laughing and joking together. We hike mountains and cook s'mores together. Our conversations are real, sometimes discussing controversial topics. They even ask how I'm doing and what's happening in my life. I no longer feel manipulated and used. There is a mutual respect. They are finding their way and taking responsibility for their lives.

A lot of time has passed since Grayson's first car wreck 15 years ago. It was a helluva ride. I was exhausted and weary but hopeful and healing. Recovery taught me a new way and a new language. I finally have answers and direction in my life that give me comfort and joy. My life today is lived in freedom, freedom from obsession. I use tools everyday that empower healthy living.

Attending 12 step meetings and working the steps, reading Al Anon literature and coffee dates with others in recovery are part of my daily life.

I now have a voice, which leads me to take care of myself physically, emotionally, and spiritually. Eating vegetables, drinking water, and walking help me physically. Prayer and meditation improve my contact with God. Journaling and phone calls help me emotionally, along with responding and not reacting, which keep me emotionally sane. I can say how I feel and what I need in all these areas of functioning. And these areas affect each other and help me to live from a principled place. Therapy groups and hobbies contribute to my well-being. And I don't plan to "graduate" from working recovery. Thank God I have a new way of living.

I will continue to live in freedom.

§

Beyond Rock Bottom (Grayson)

The life I live today does not share a lot in common with the life that I lived before coming into the program of Alcoholics Anonymous and working the Twelve Steps. The difference is staggering. What is amazing to me is that I am in a sturdy place to be able to help others. I find myself automatically saying "yes" when someone asks for a ride or if they can borrow a couple of bucks. This is coming from a guy who used to keep score of everything and wouldn't "give" anything away. I have had a change of personality and I used to believe that was impossible.

I am comfortable in my own skin today. I like the man I have worked to become. Last week I went to a meeting and was greeted by familiar faces, smiles and hugs. This was not at all like my first meeting in Salt Lake City. I went to that first meeting because I had to. I was convinced that it would save my life and I had no other choice in the matter. I went because people told me to go. I introduced myself to people because it was slightly less awkward than avoiding eye contact. I hated it because it was so uncomfortable. I wanted to burst out of my skin. I would see people having conversations and laughing and that would make everything worse because I didn't feel like they looked. I kept doing it. I introduced myself to more people. I shared at meetings no matter how uncomfortable it was. I was inspired by what I heard in meetings so I did what people suggested. I wanted to be sober and I wanted to be comfortable. I am surprised at how quickly I became comfortable in my own skin. I could finally breathe in a room full of people. Now, most of the time, it comes naturally and I find myself initiating conversations - something that was very hard for me to do before I got sober. I was convinced that I simply did not have the ability to be social.

Last week I went to the gun range with my good friend, JP, the admissions director at the treatment center I attended. We have become good friends. We spent about an hour and a half at the gun range. It was a cool afternoon and we had a great view of the mountains surrounding Salt Lake City. We didn't talk much. It wasn't uncomfortable. We had our ear protection in and only communicated what was necessary to set up and retrieve our targets. I enjoyed being there with him and did not feel the need to fill the quiet space with conversation. I was not trying to figure out what he was thinking. I was just there, shooting guns and enjoying the moment. Later that day, we went back to his house and played Xbox in his living room while our dogs lay on the floor. He received a call from someone who was interested in checking into Legacy Outdoor Adventures Treatment center. Then it hit me. I was once that guy on the other end of the line. Not too long ago, I was in tears talking to JP about how scared I was. I wanted a way out, but I didn't know what to do. The biggest resource I had then was a guy I had never met who I believed had my best interest in mind and was going to do everything he could to get me into treatment. I was clueless as to how to live a fulfilling life and the thought of using for the rest of my life brought me to tears every time. I absolutely hated who I was and I was in constant emotional pain. I wanted a way out but I didn't know what to do. Now as he was taking this phone call from another helpless individual, I was relaxing on a big leather couch with dogs resting at my feet, playing Battlefield 1 on the Xbox. I had developed a meaningful relationship with this man that I respect and wanted to be like. My truck was parked outside and I had a date with a young lady at a Thai restaurant in about an hour. I had no need to get high before the date, because I had become comfortable showing up sober. I am confident in my ability to have a conversation so I don't need to drink a couple beers beforehand. With the help of many people, I have managed to put a life together that I am proud of.

Just recently I had plans with a lady I had been dating. She was going to come over and make dinner with me. We had plans to do this since the previous week. I already had bought vegetables and chicken to make stir-fry. It was a Saturday night. Five minutes before she was to arrive, she texted me. She said something along the lines of: "My friend just texted me and wants to have a girls' night out. I think I am going to go out with them. Would you hate me if I did?". In the past, I would have replied "yea, no problem we can do it some other time." This time was different. I didn't want to spend time with someone who was not willing to honor their commitments to me, no matter how small. Instead of telling her it was ok and we would do something another time, I said, "hate is a strong word, but I would be upset and it is not ok with me for you to cancel under these circumstances." She ended up coming over after all and we had a great time. I was so goddamn proud of myself for establishing some boundaries. I have heard people say that we teach people how we want to be treated and I think this is a great example of that.

I have something that a lot of drug addicts and alcoholics would die for. I have developed a spiritual way of living and as a result, the mental obsession of using has left me. I have ambition. I gave up drugs and alcohol and what I got in return was a life I thought was not an option for me. I did not think being content in sobriety was possible. I didn't think a spiritual life was possible. I am so glad I was wrong. I keep my Sundays free so I can sponsor other guys in the program and pass along what was so freely given to me. The more I do this, the simpler it gets. I sit and read the Big Book with them and listen to all sorts of complex problems. The answer is the same for all the guys I sponsor. They all have to do the same exact thing (work recovery) to get the relief that I found. The relief that I used to get from drugs and alcohol. This new life allows me to sleep at night and laugh during the day. I try not to think about it too much, but it amazes me that such complex mental problems can be solved with such simplicity.

Most, if not all of my problems, have been resolved as a result of working the 12 steps with a sponsor. I am excited to share what I found with other men in the program. I am proud to be of service. I have a very different attitude toward life and it is a thrill to be a part of other people's recovery.

I have found a meaningful and fulfilling life beyond rock bottom.

§

Thanks for reading our story. We enjoyed the whole process of working together. It has been healing and cathartic for us as we wrote out our pain and resolutions, finding peace in our individual journey and connection together. Our hope for you is for physical, emotional and spiritual health. Feel free to contact us (pattys123@hotmail.com or gsmith@prescott.edu). We would love to hear from you. We wish you every blessing as you live your life.

ABOUT THE AUTHORS

Grayson Smith
Grayson lives with his dog, Lady, in Salt Lake City where he works construction. He is attending school and is pursuing a civil engineering degree from the University of Utah. He stays busy climbing, skiing, and is active in Alcoholics Anonymous (AA).

Patty Smith
Patty is married to Buddy Smith. They live in Columbia, South Carolina, where they raised three kids. Patty is involved in Al-Anon and other 12-step groups. She is a health coach, having received her training from IIN (Institute for Integrative Nutrition). She will be a first-time grandma this summer.

Made in the USA
Columbia, SC
16 July 2018